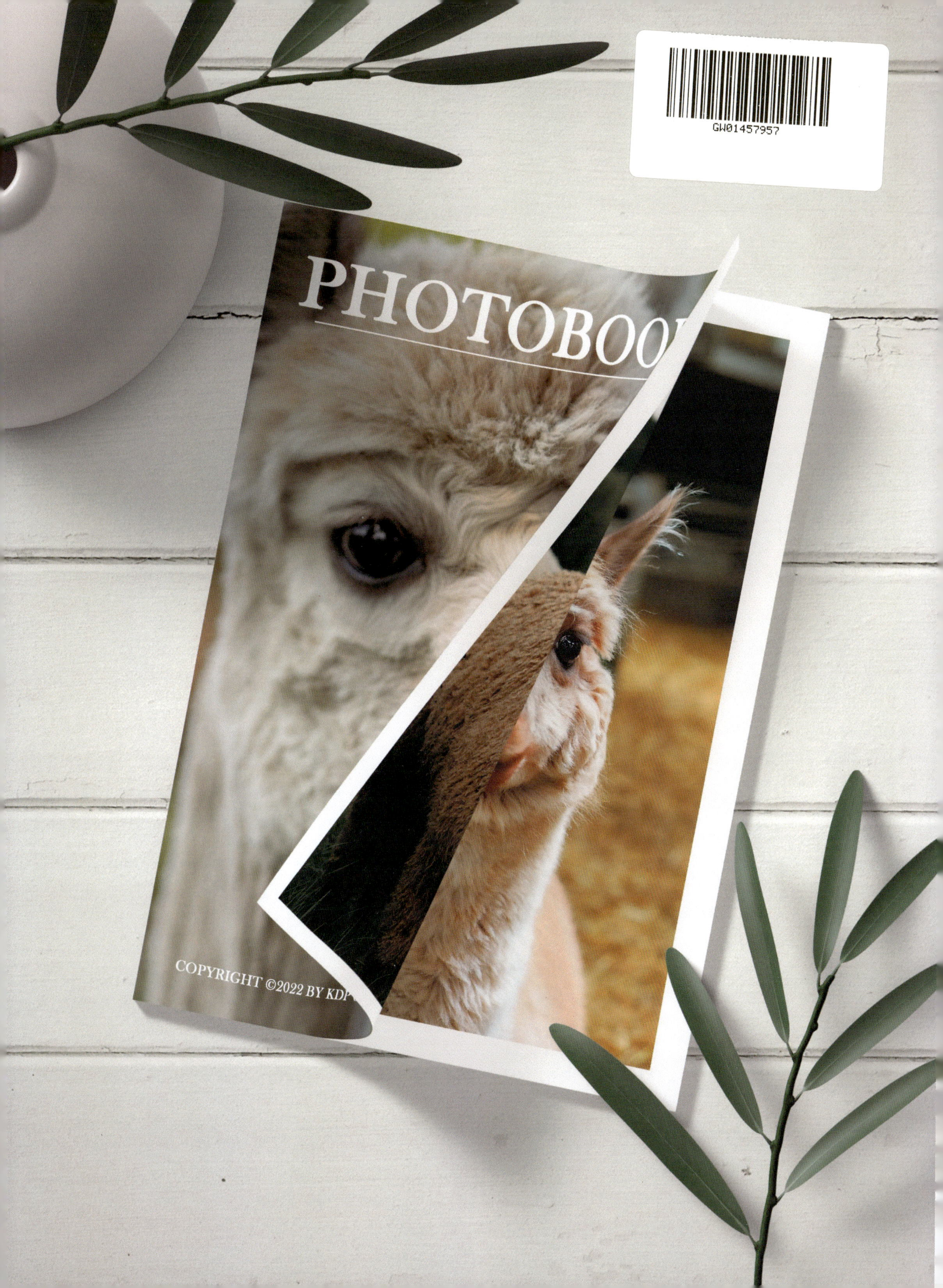
PHOTOBOO
COPYRIGHT ©2022 BY KDP

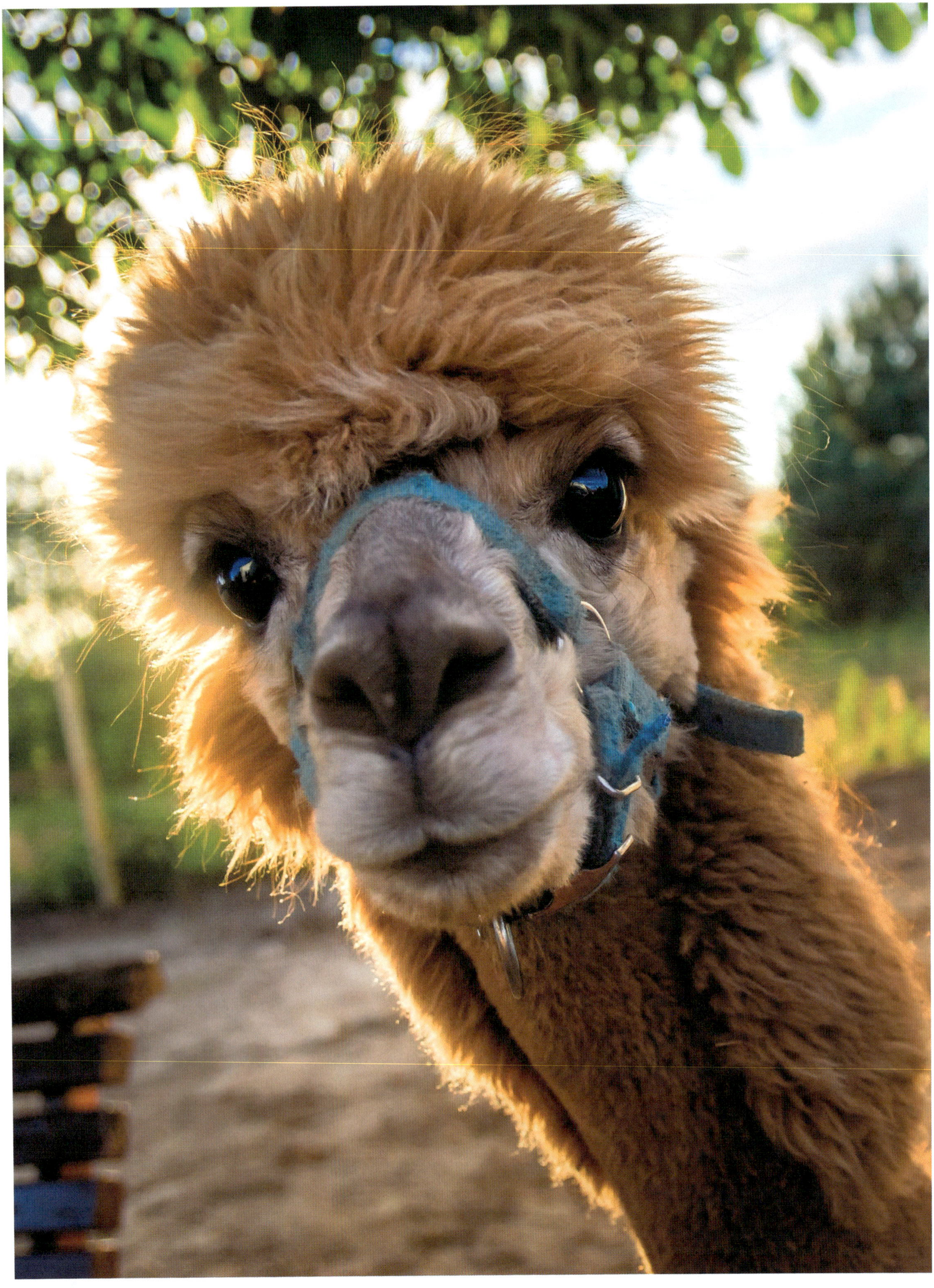

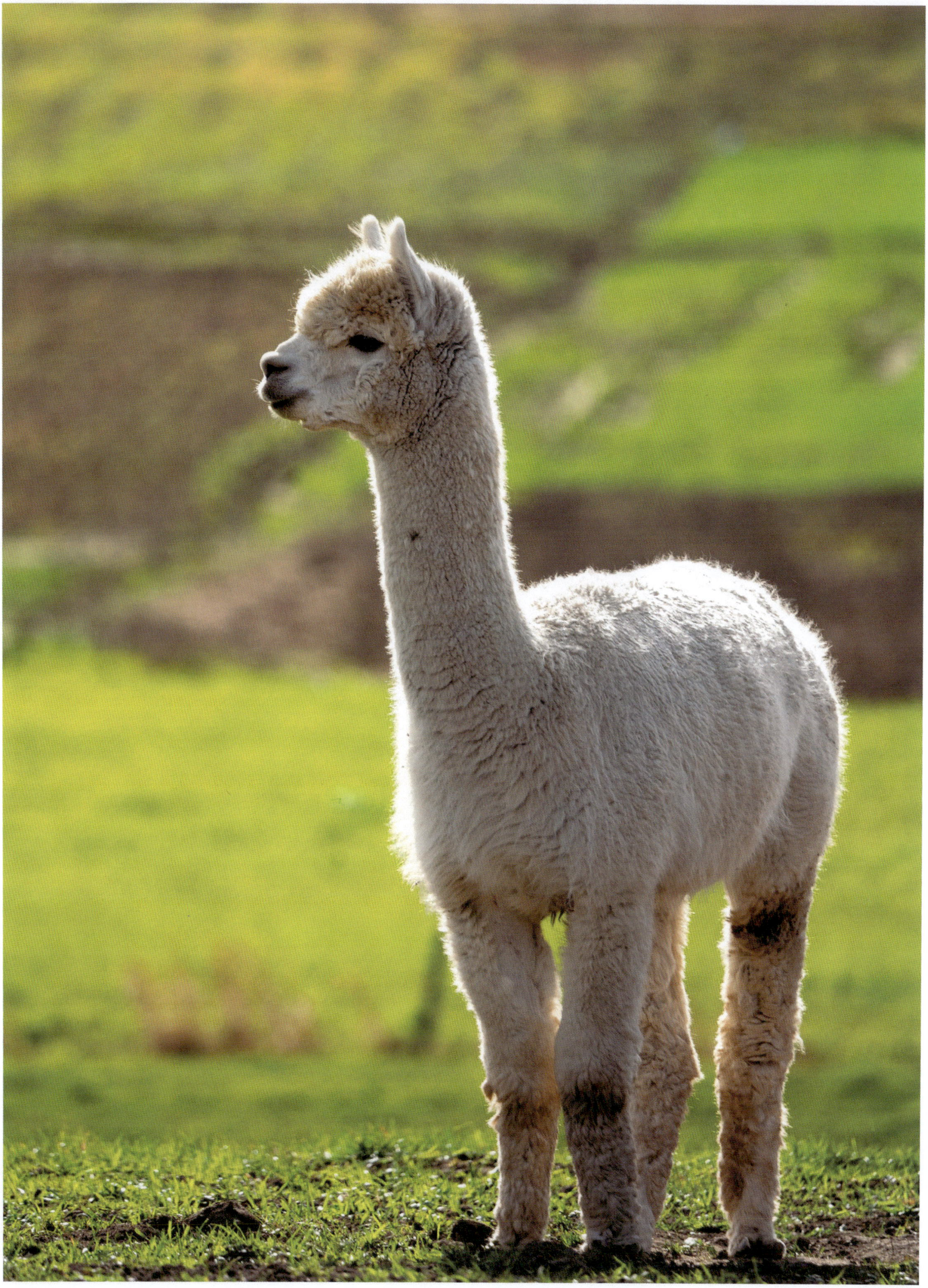

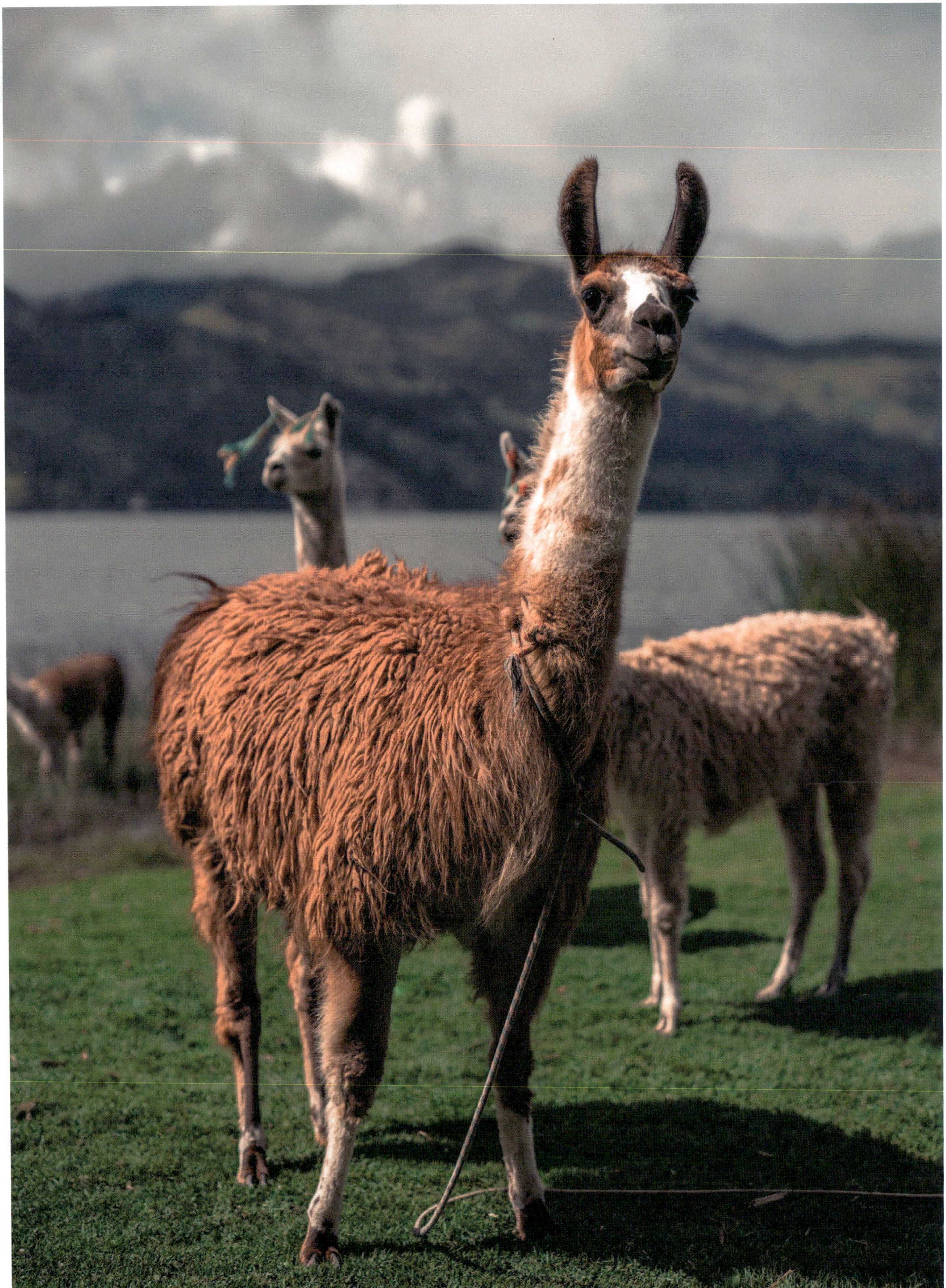

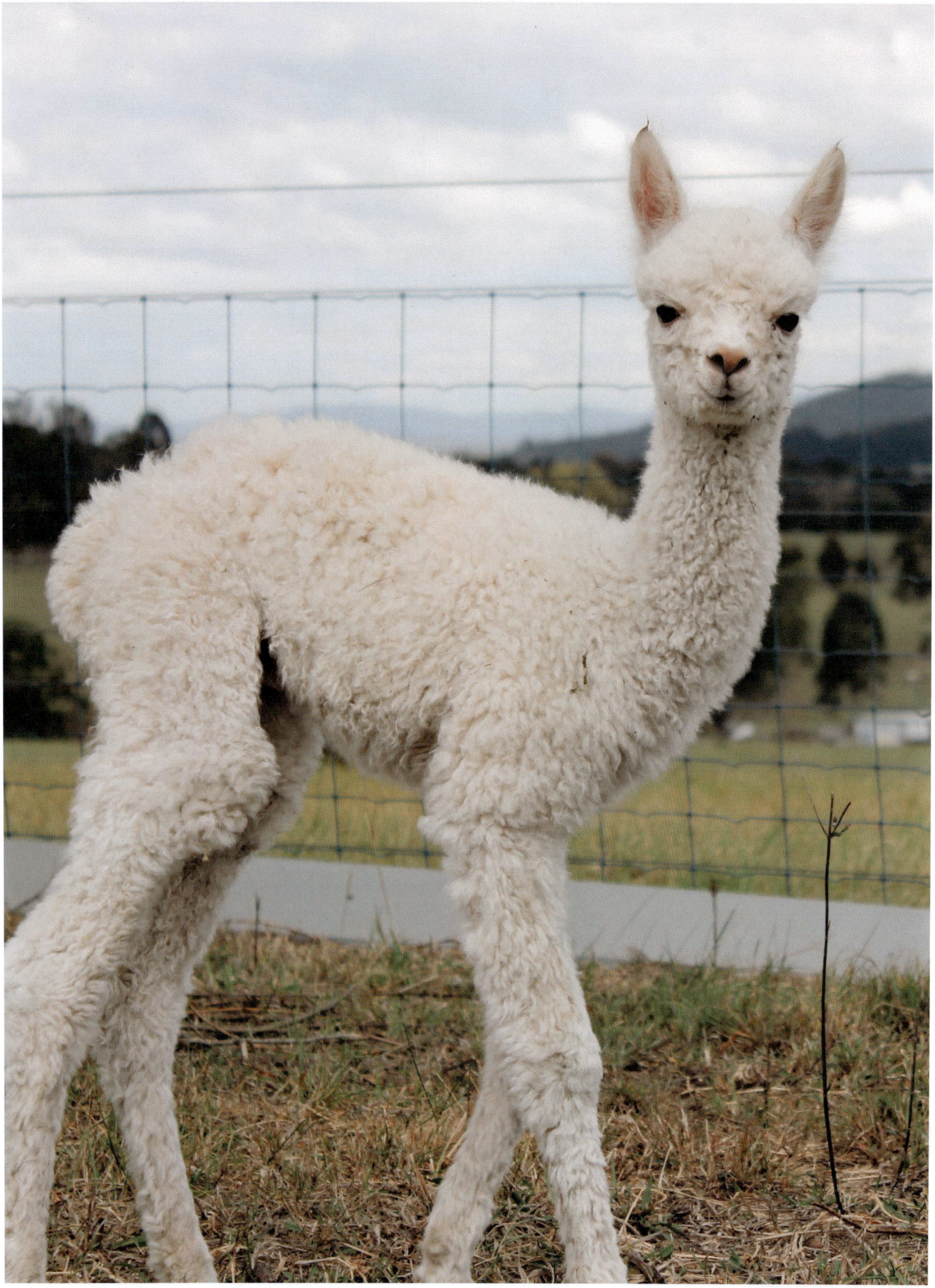

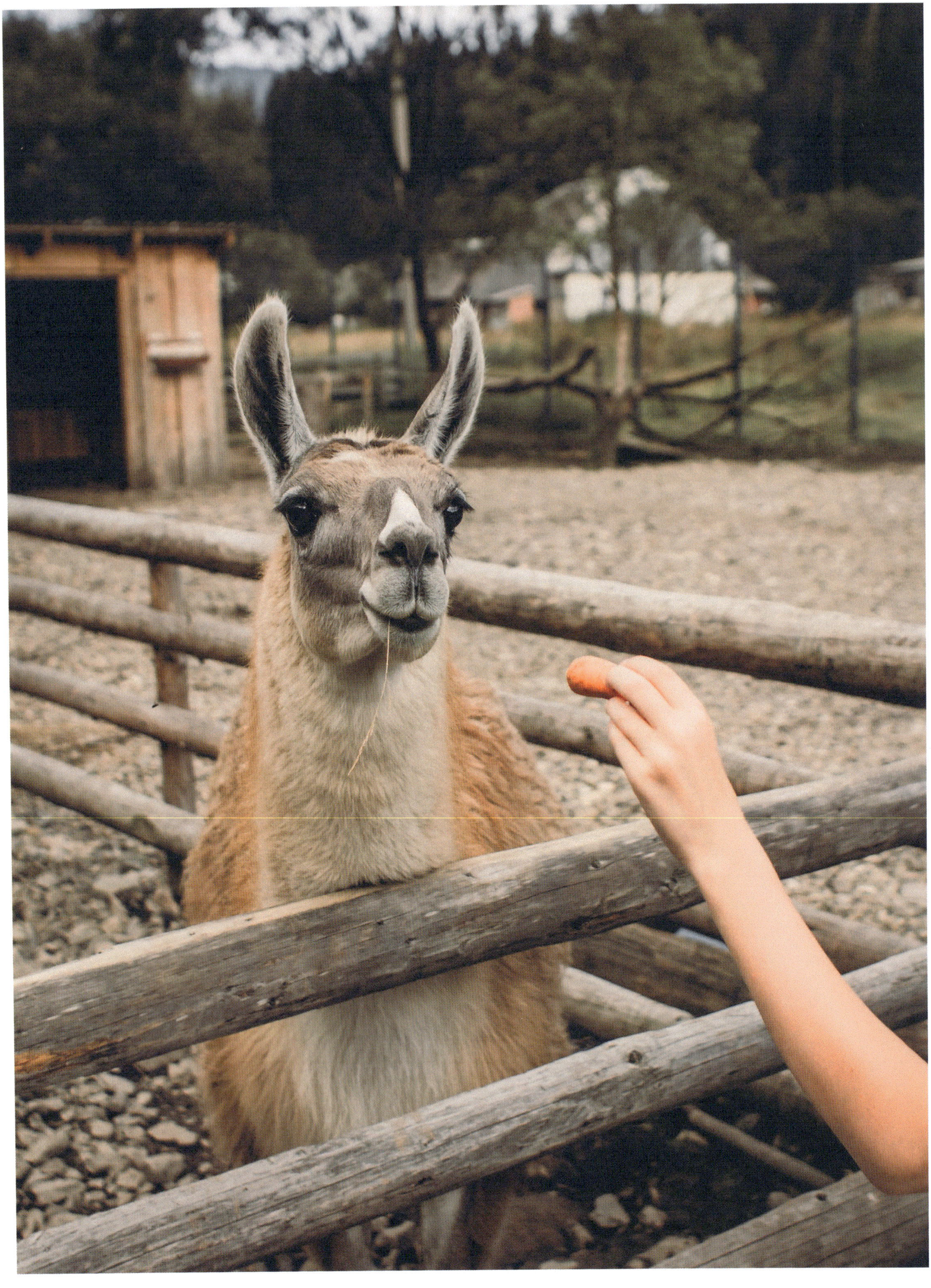

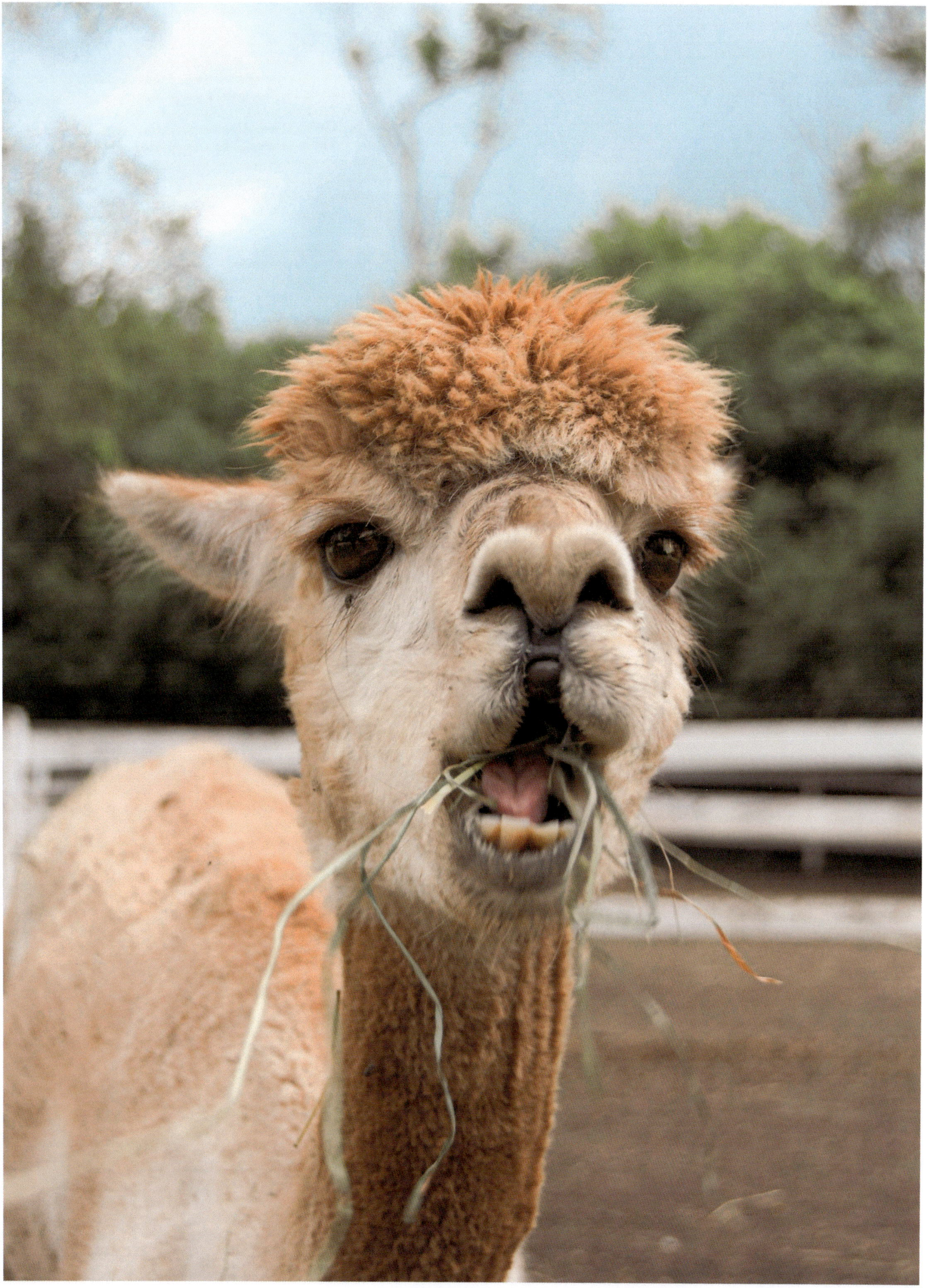

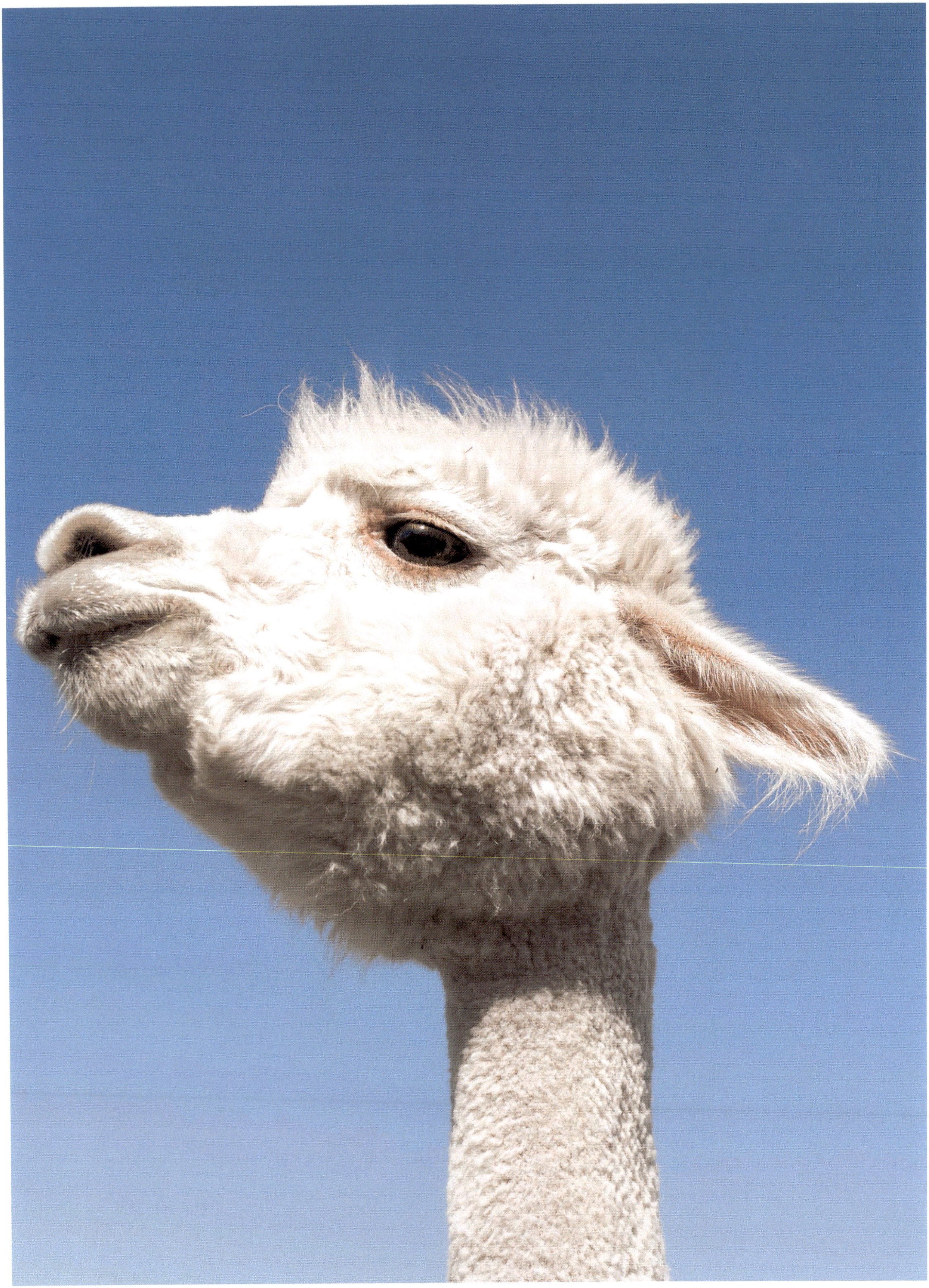

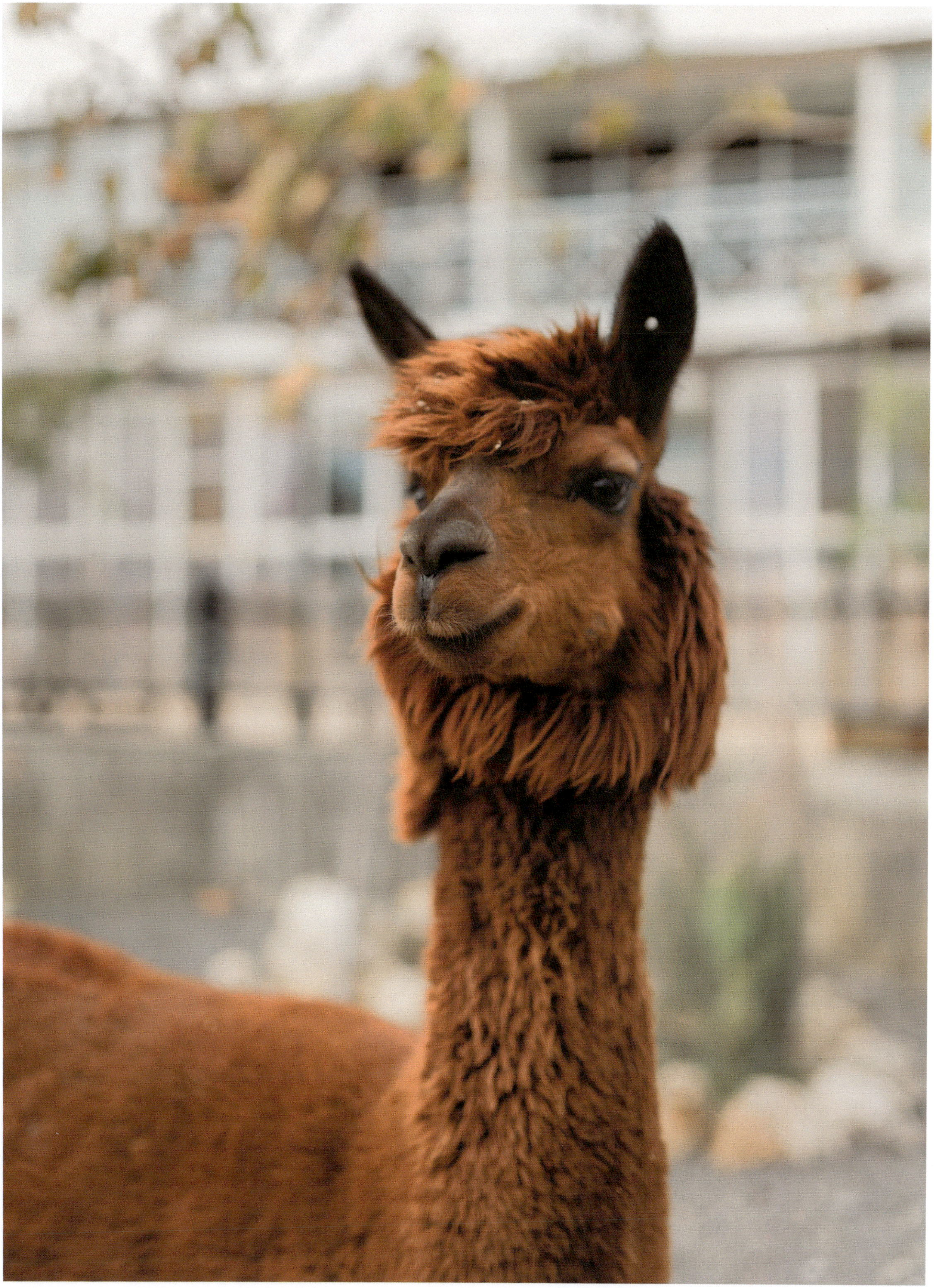

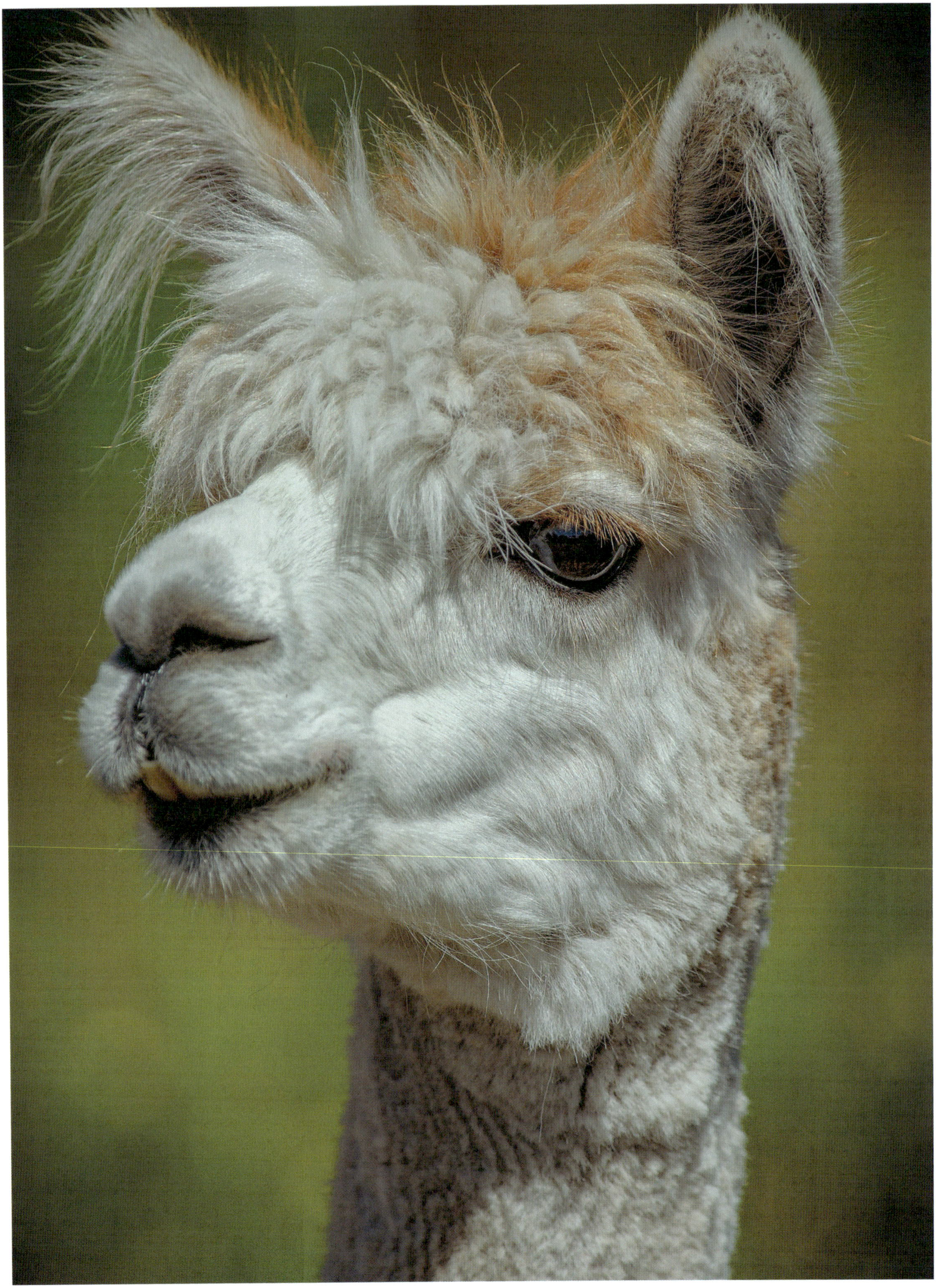

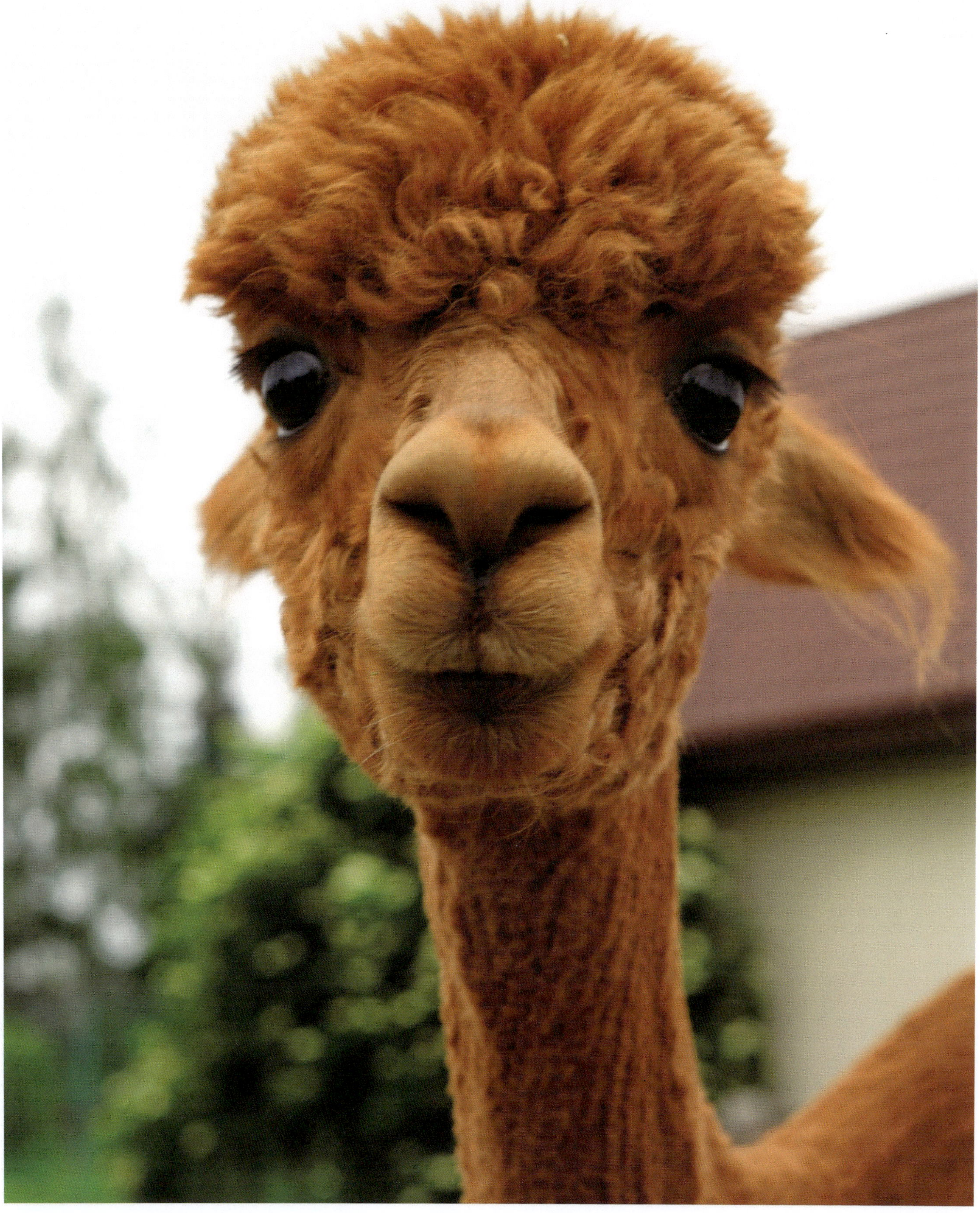

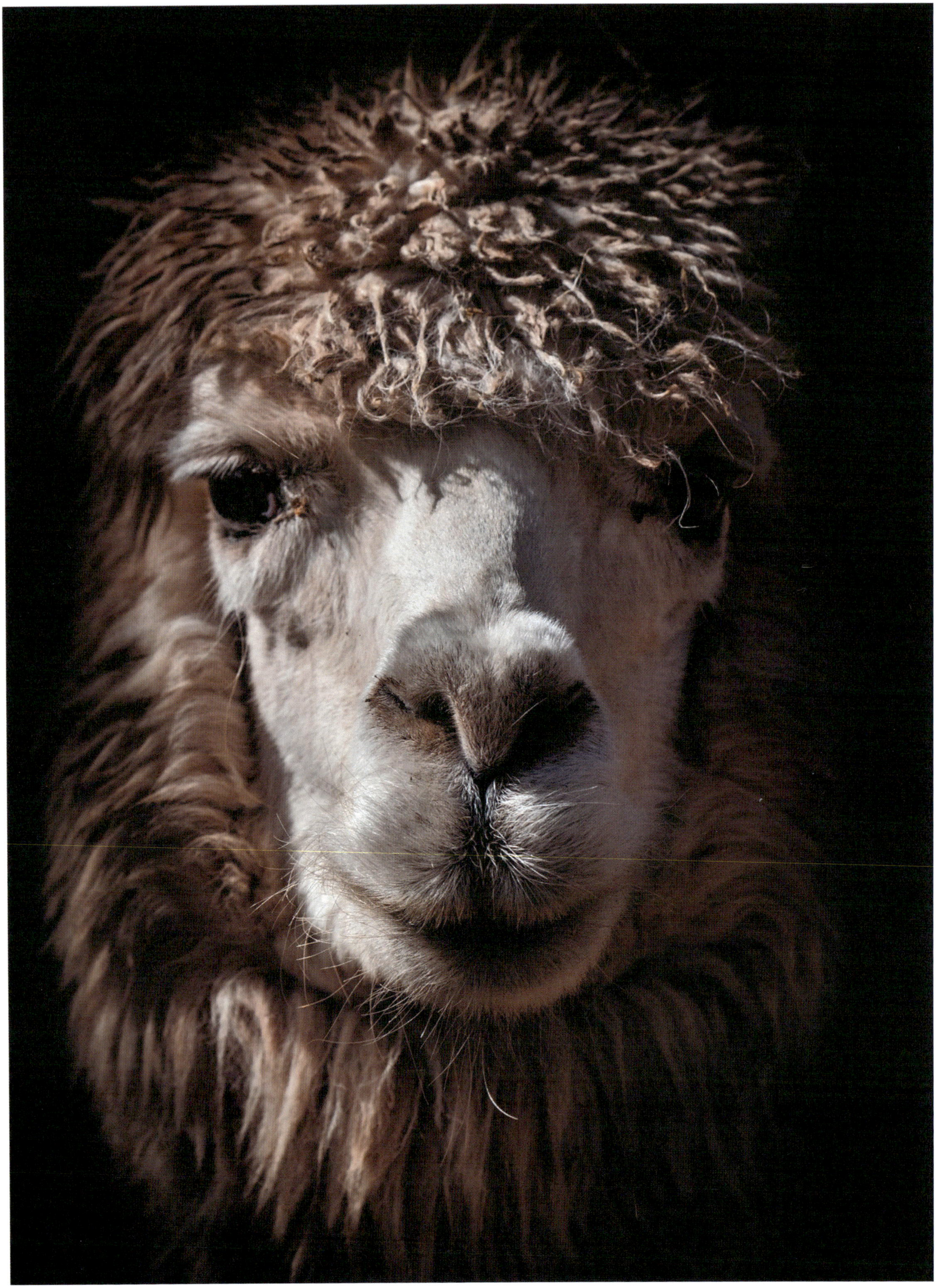

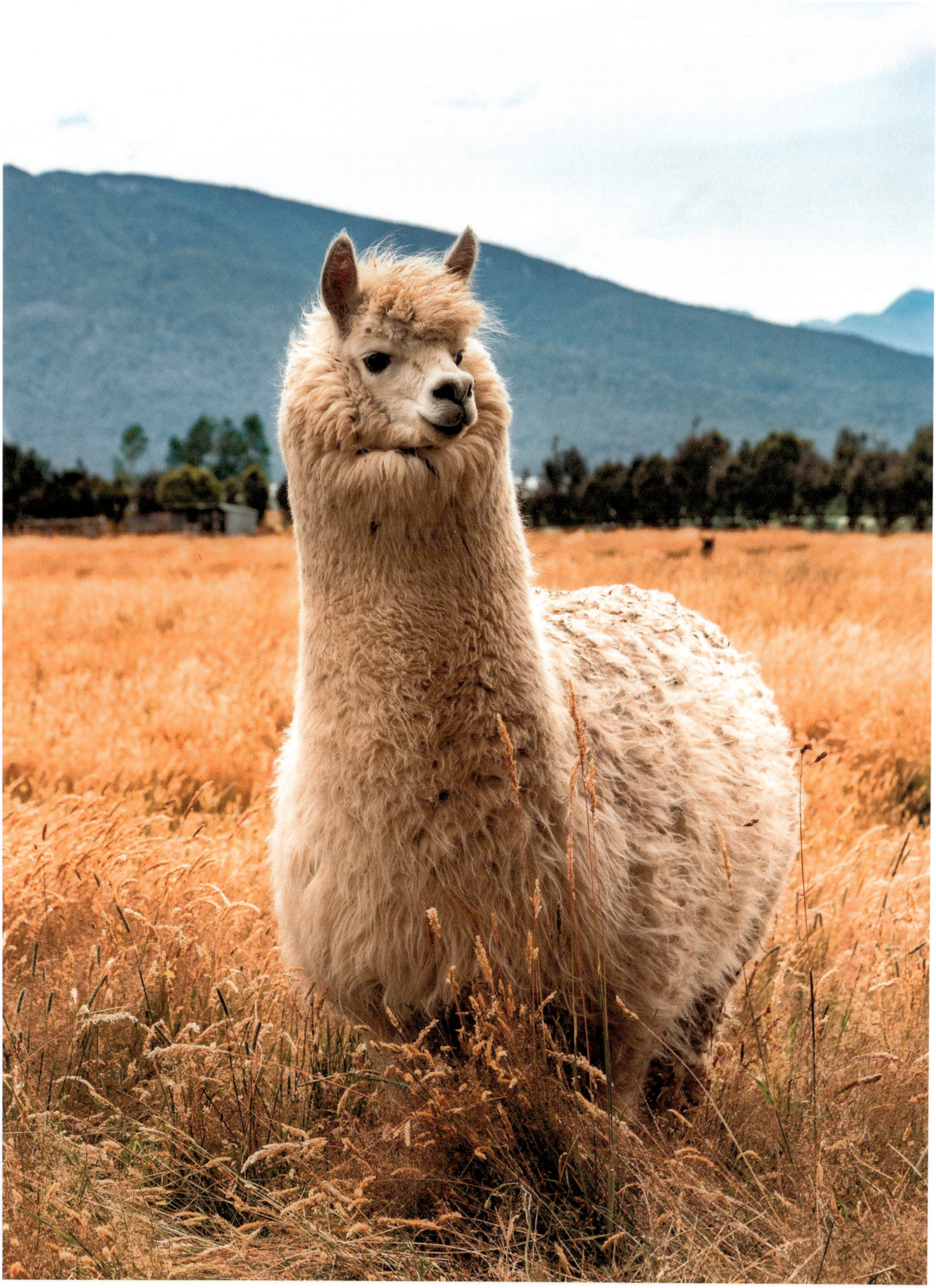

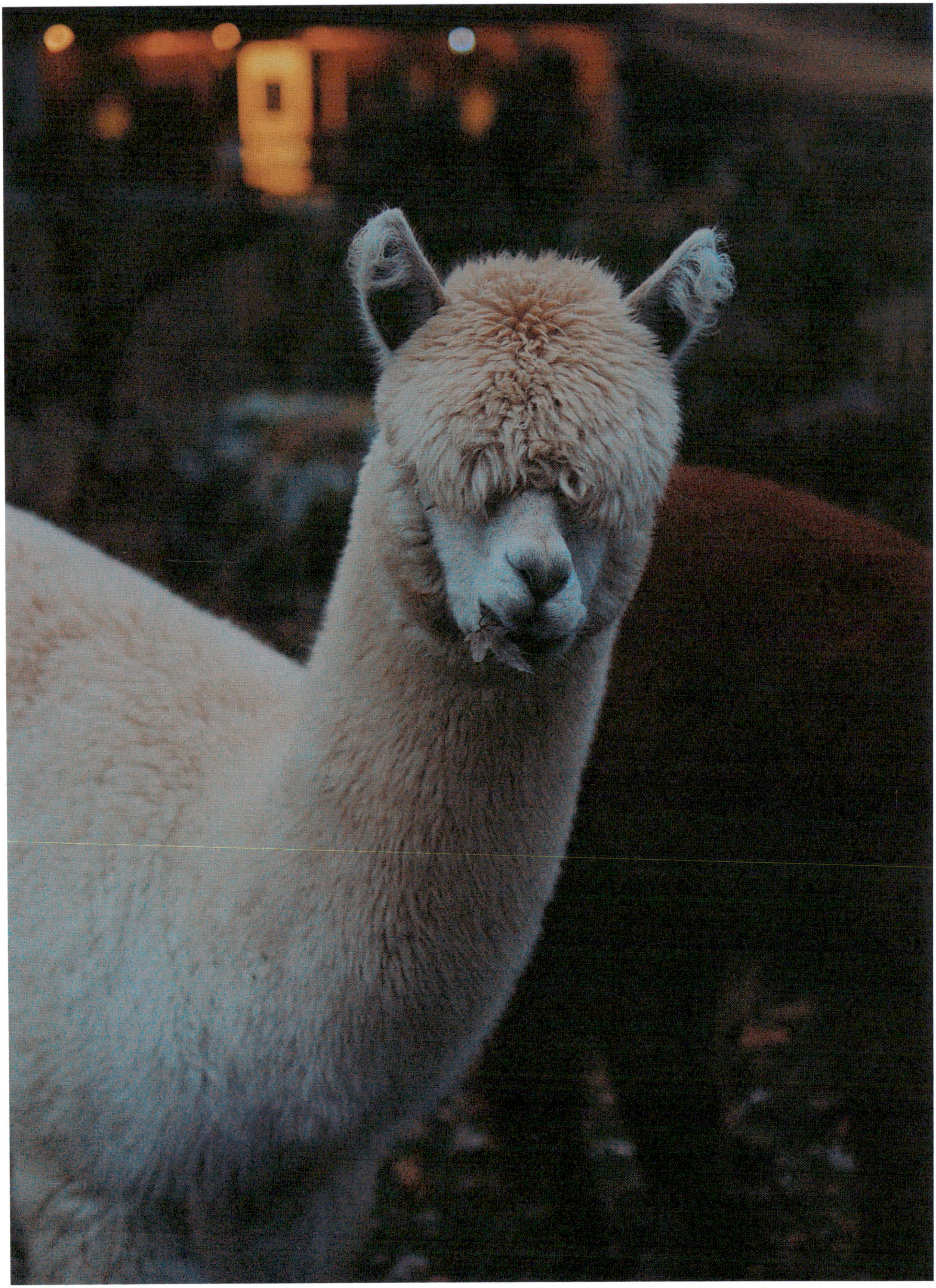

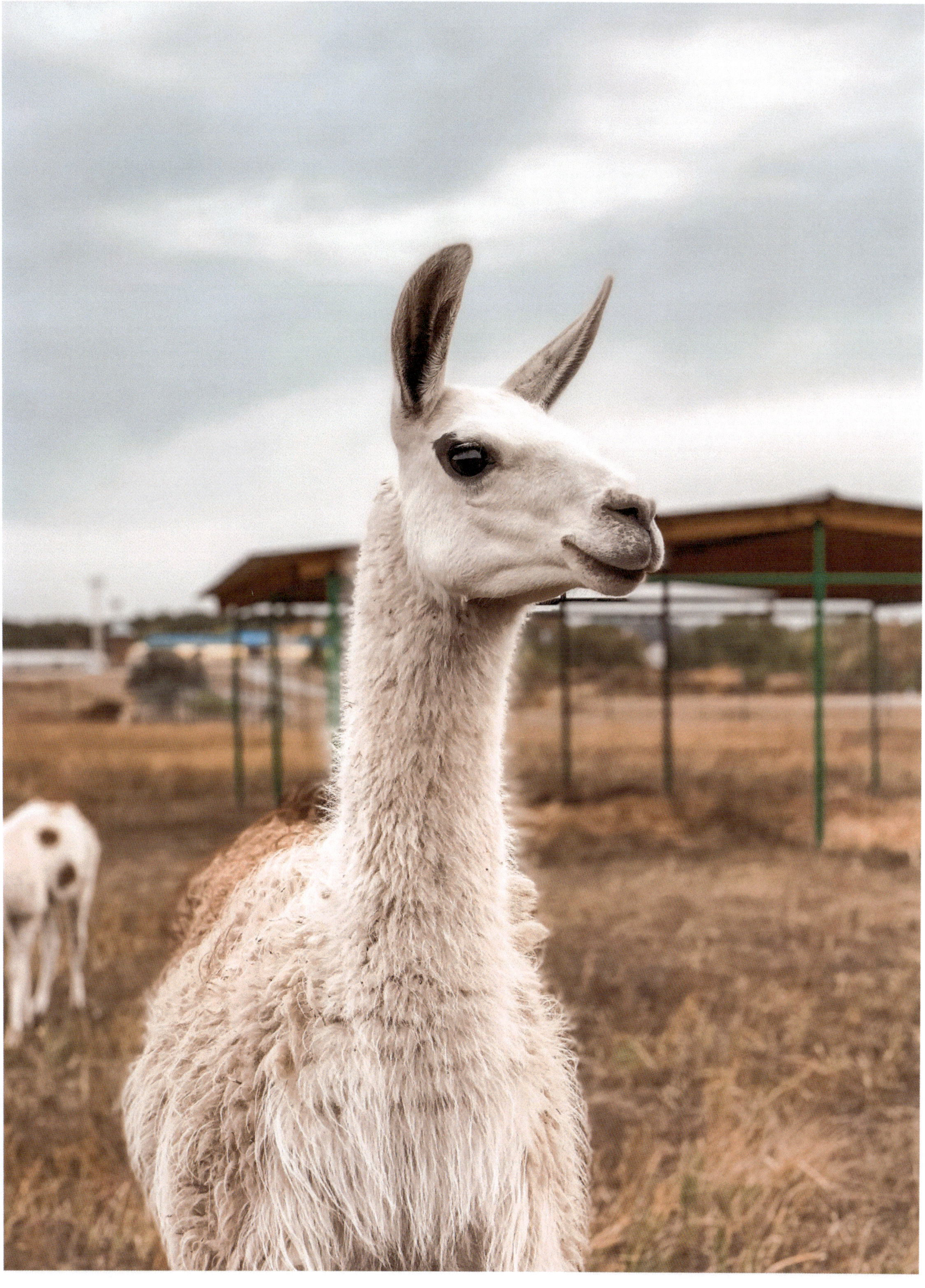

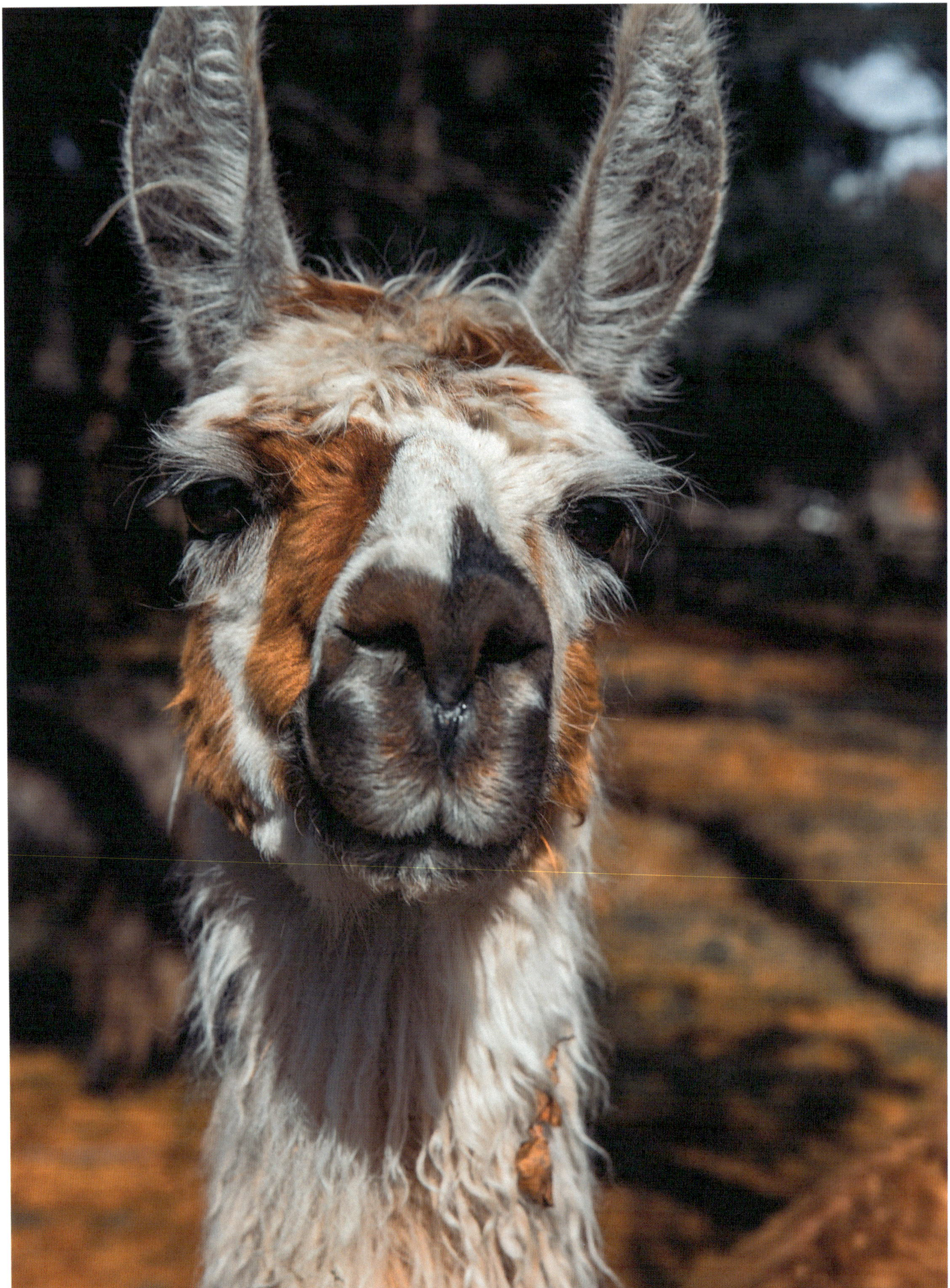

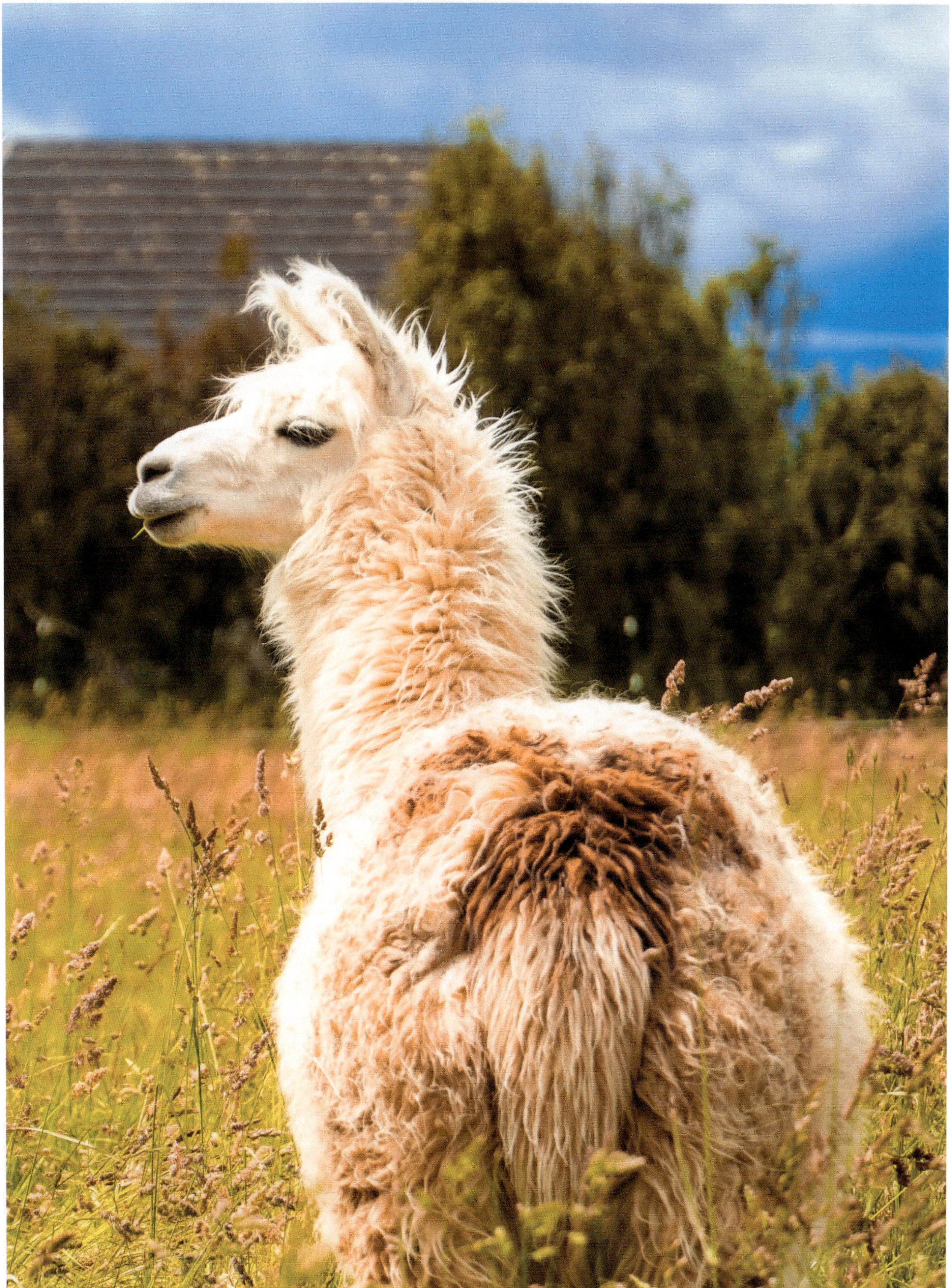

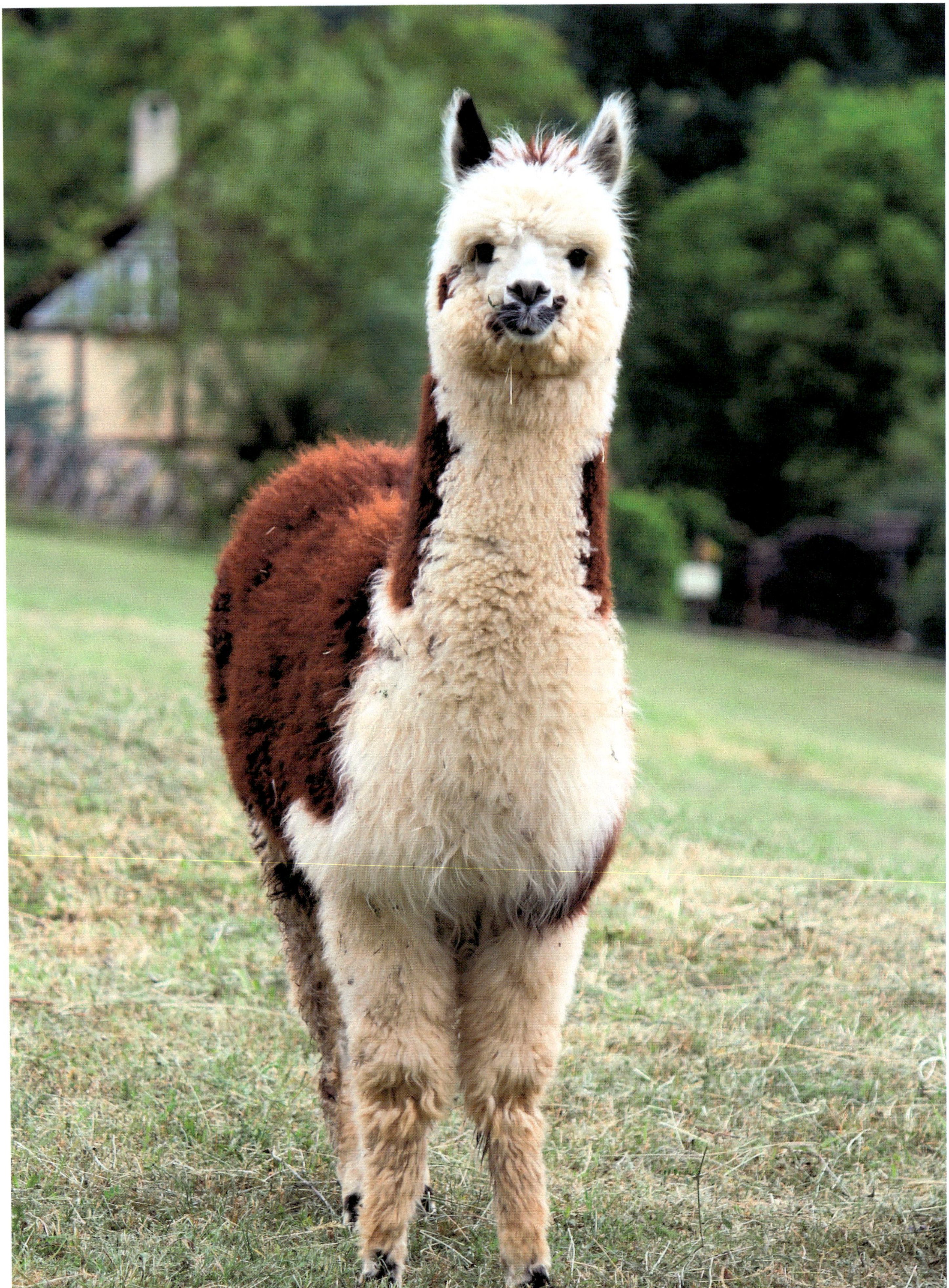

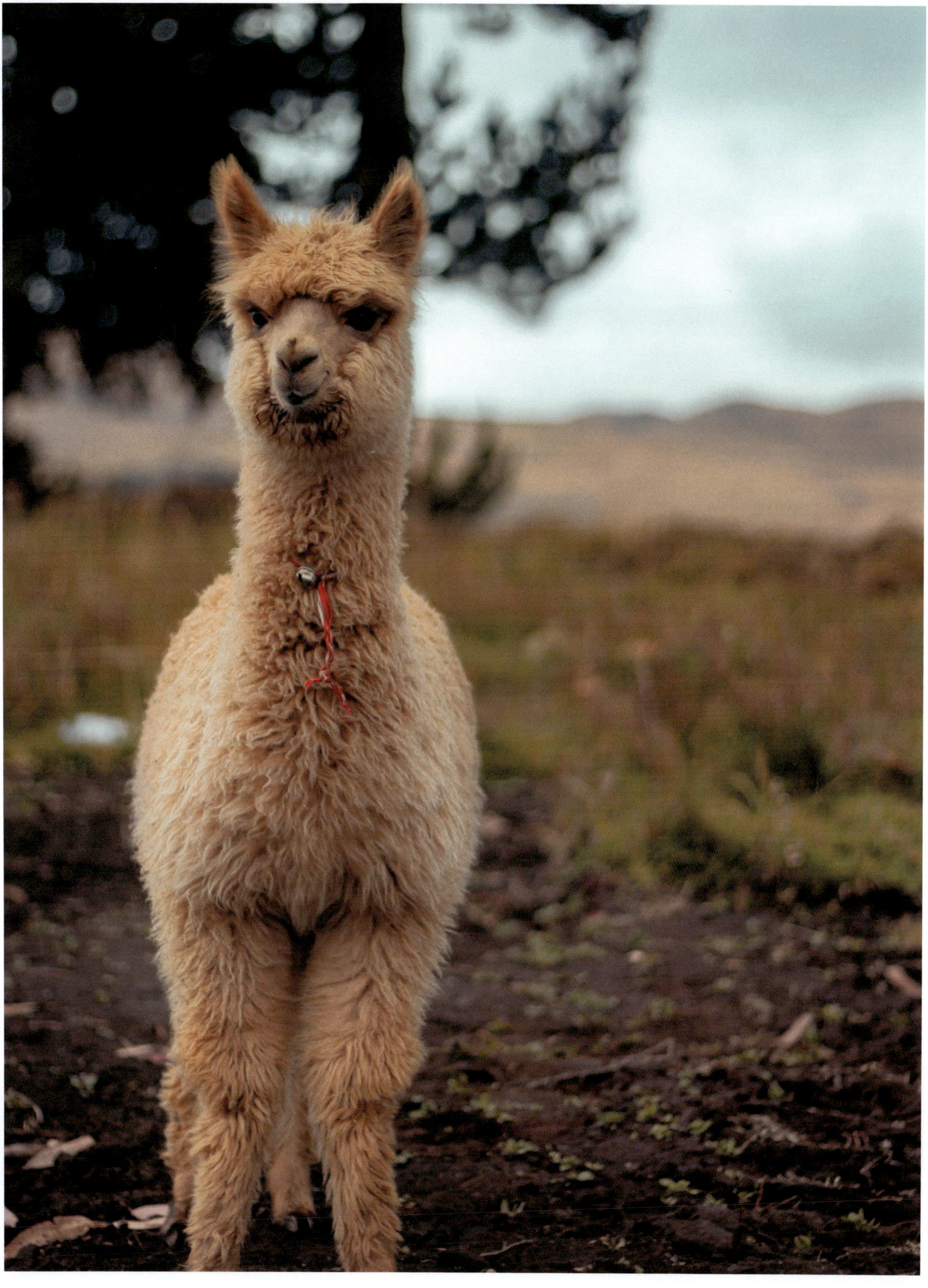

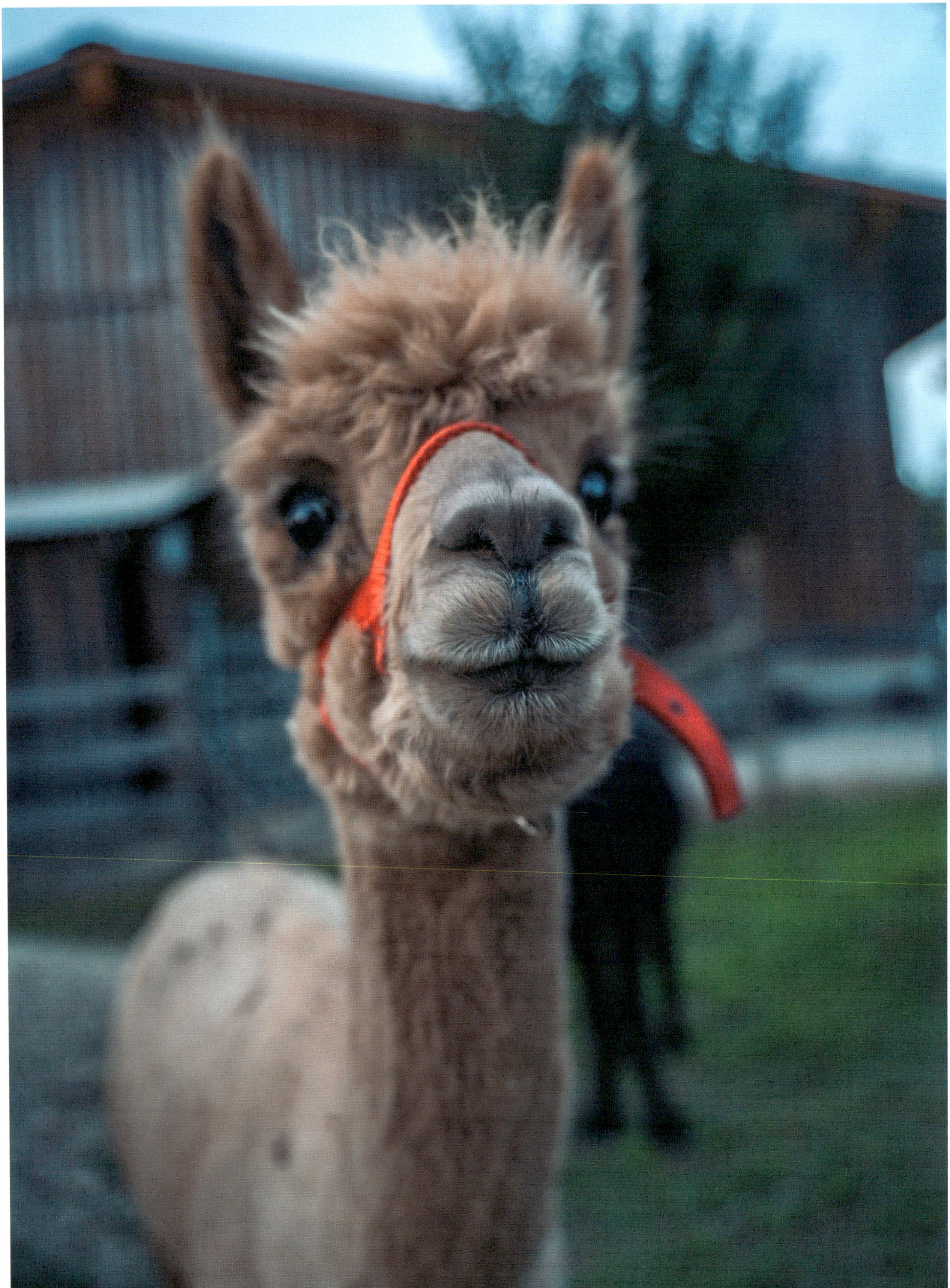

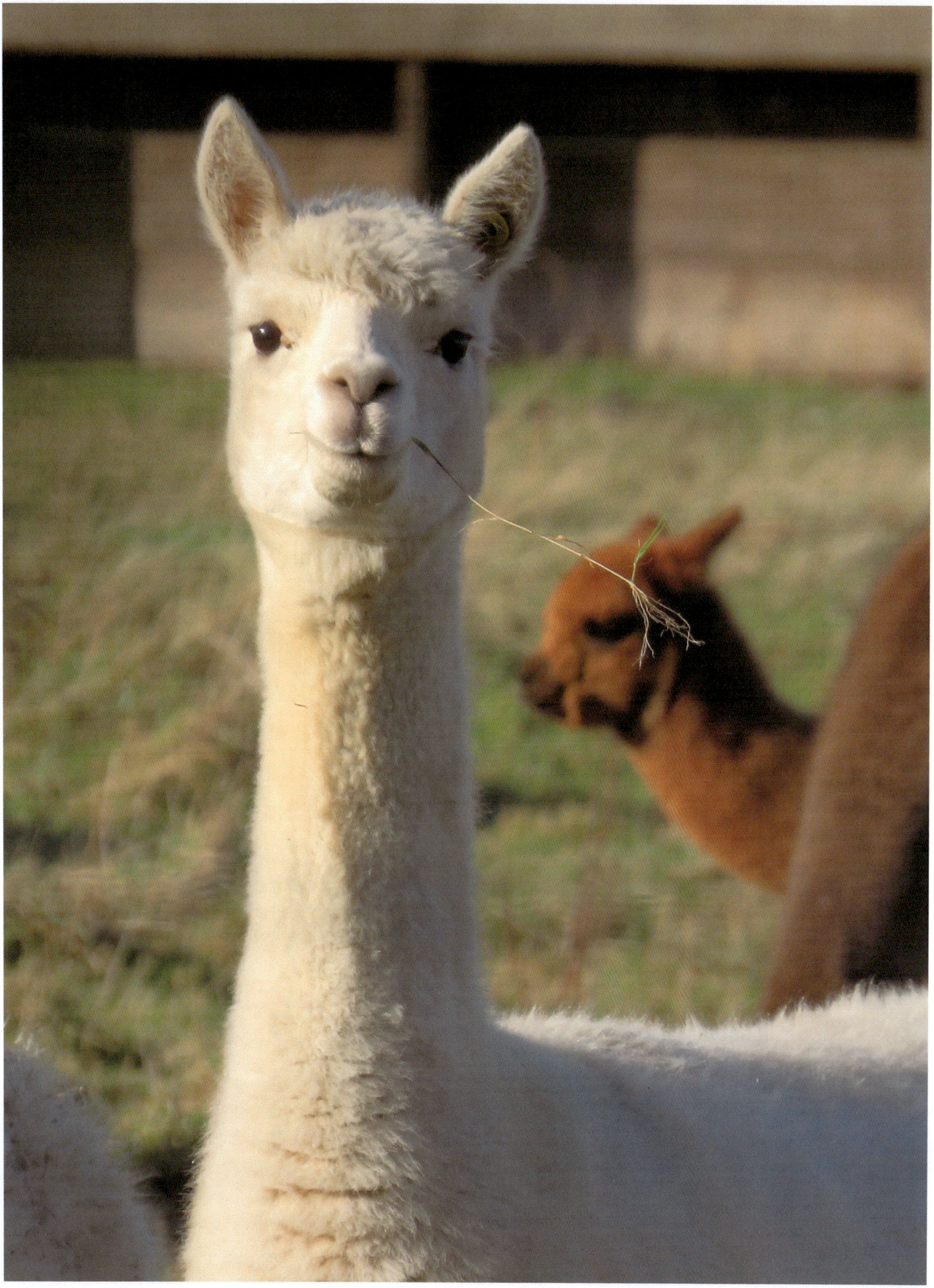

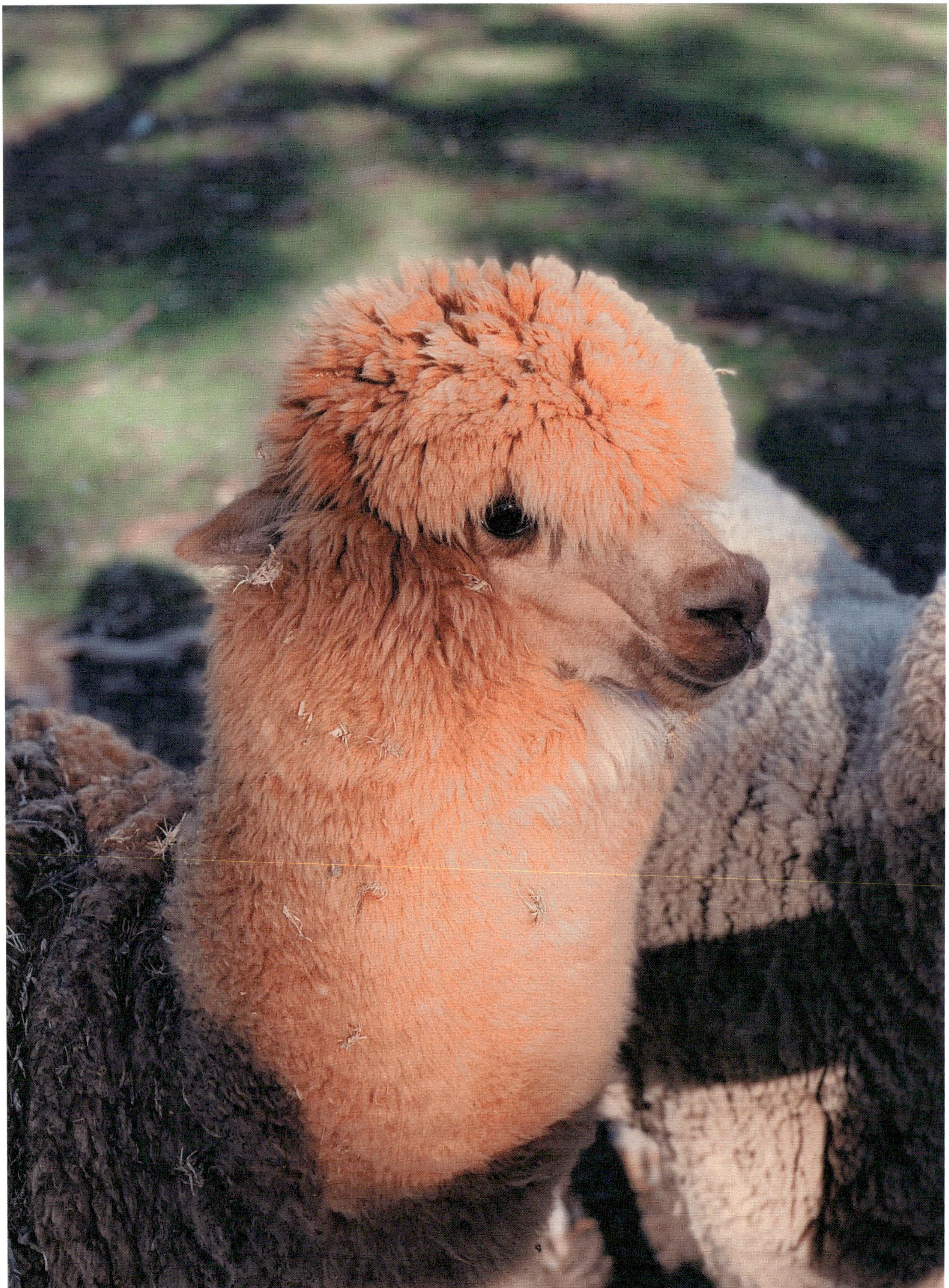

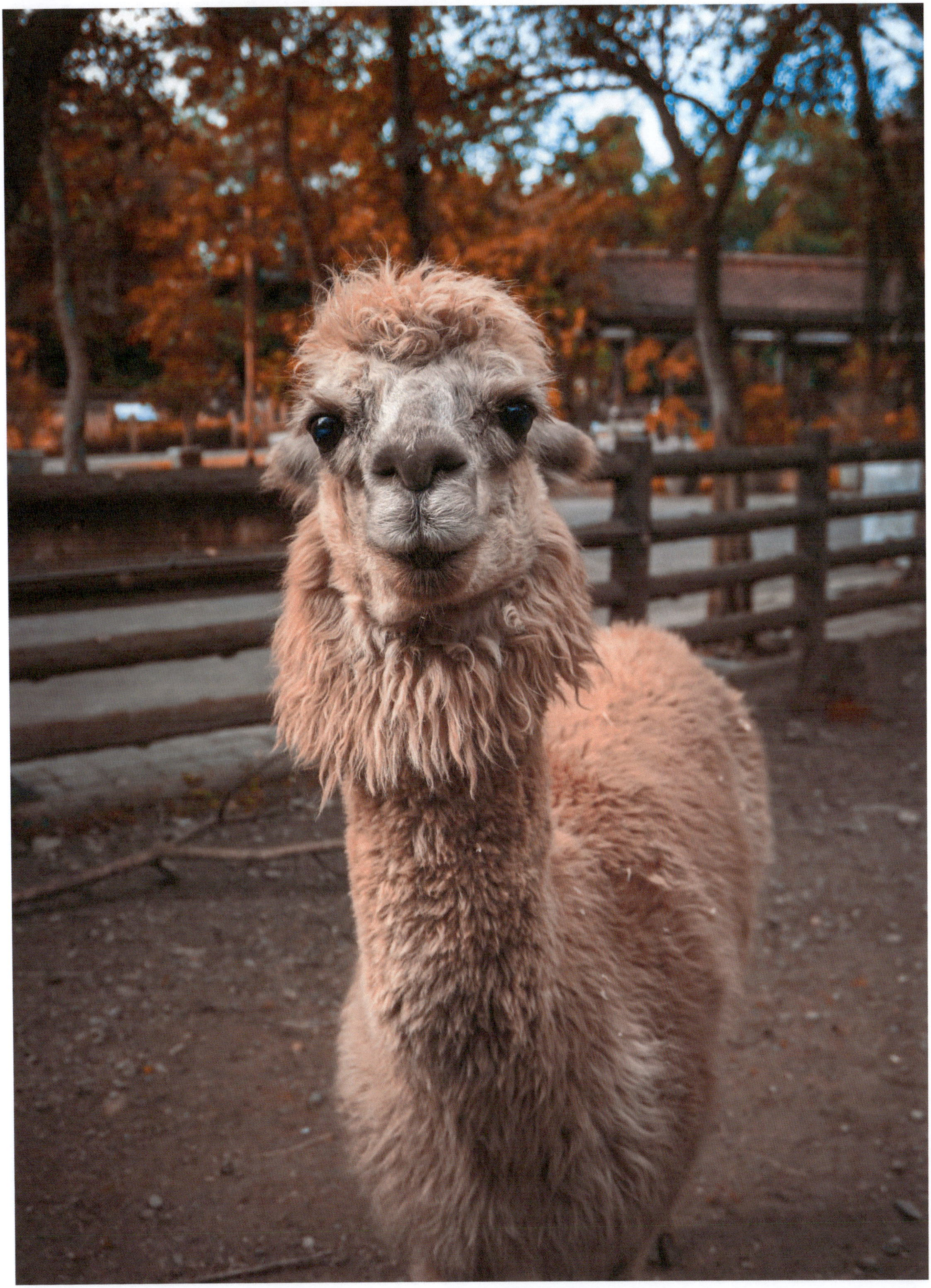

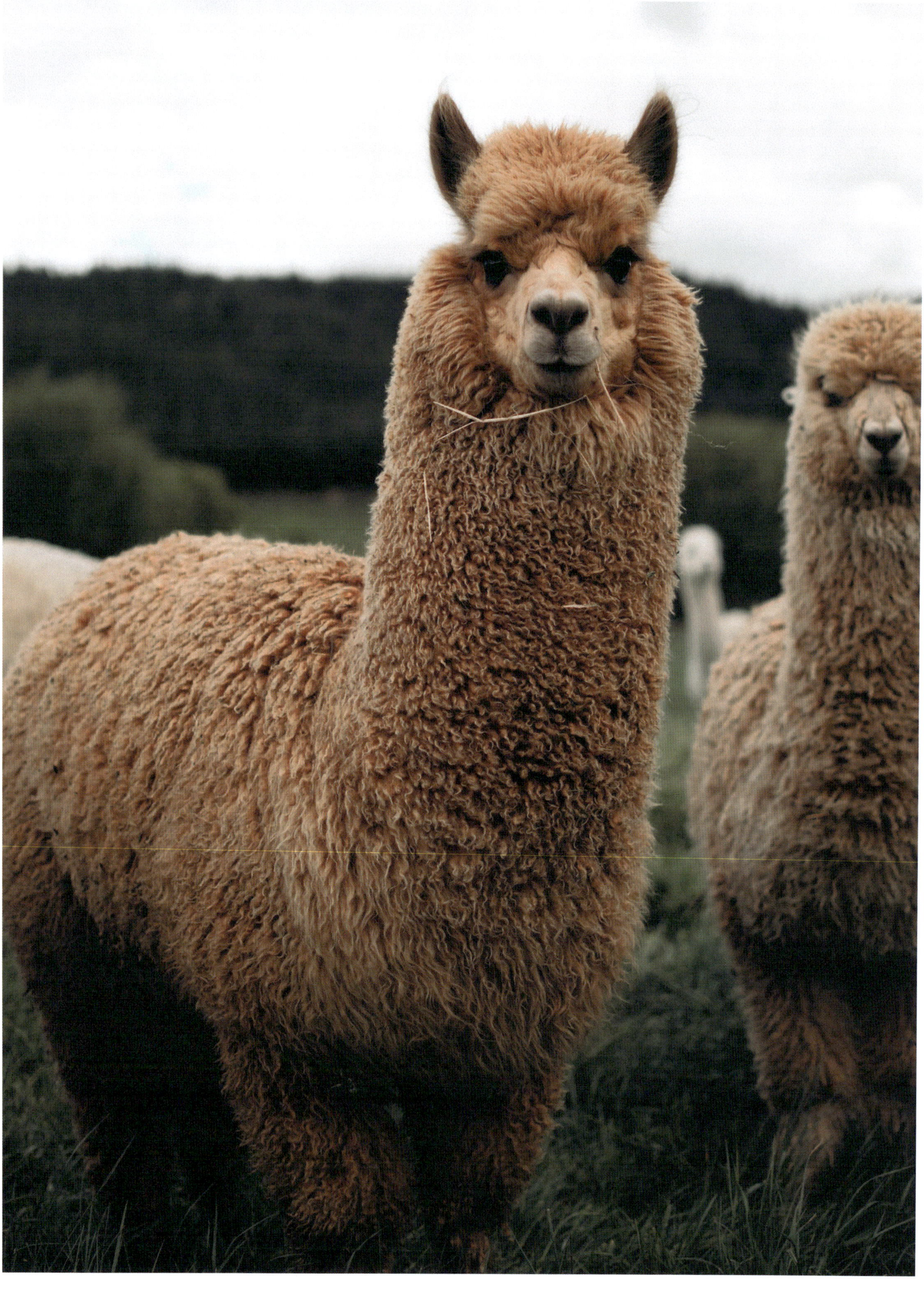

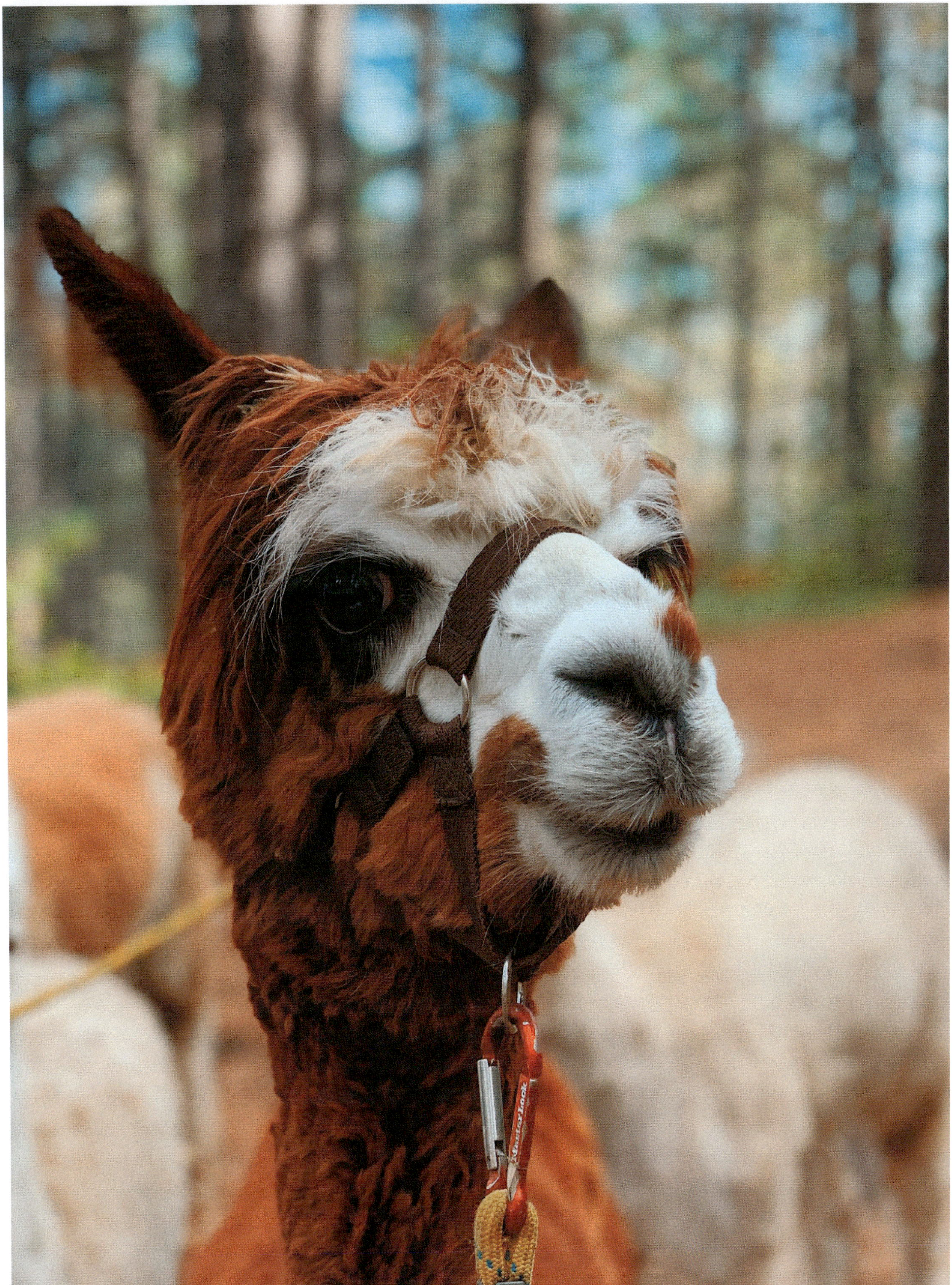

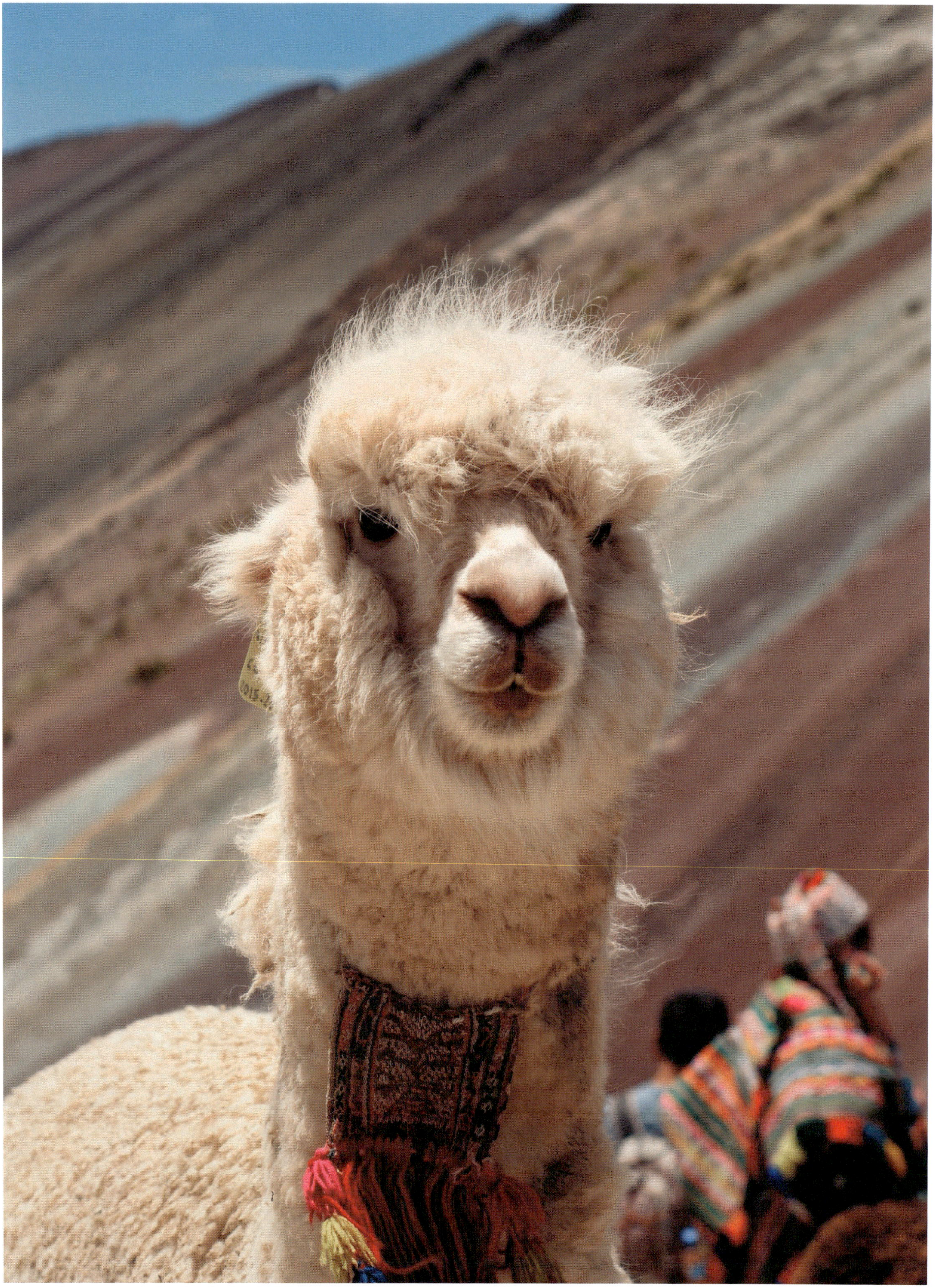

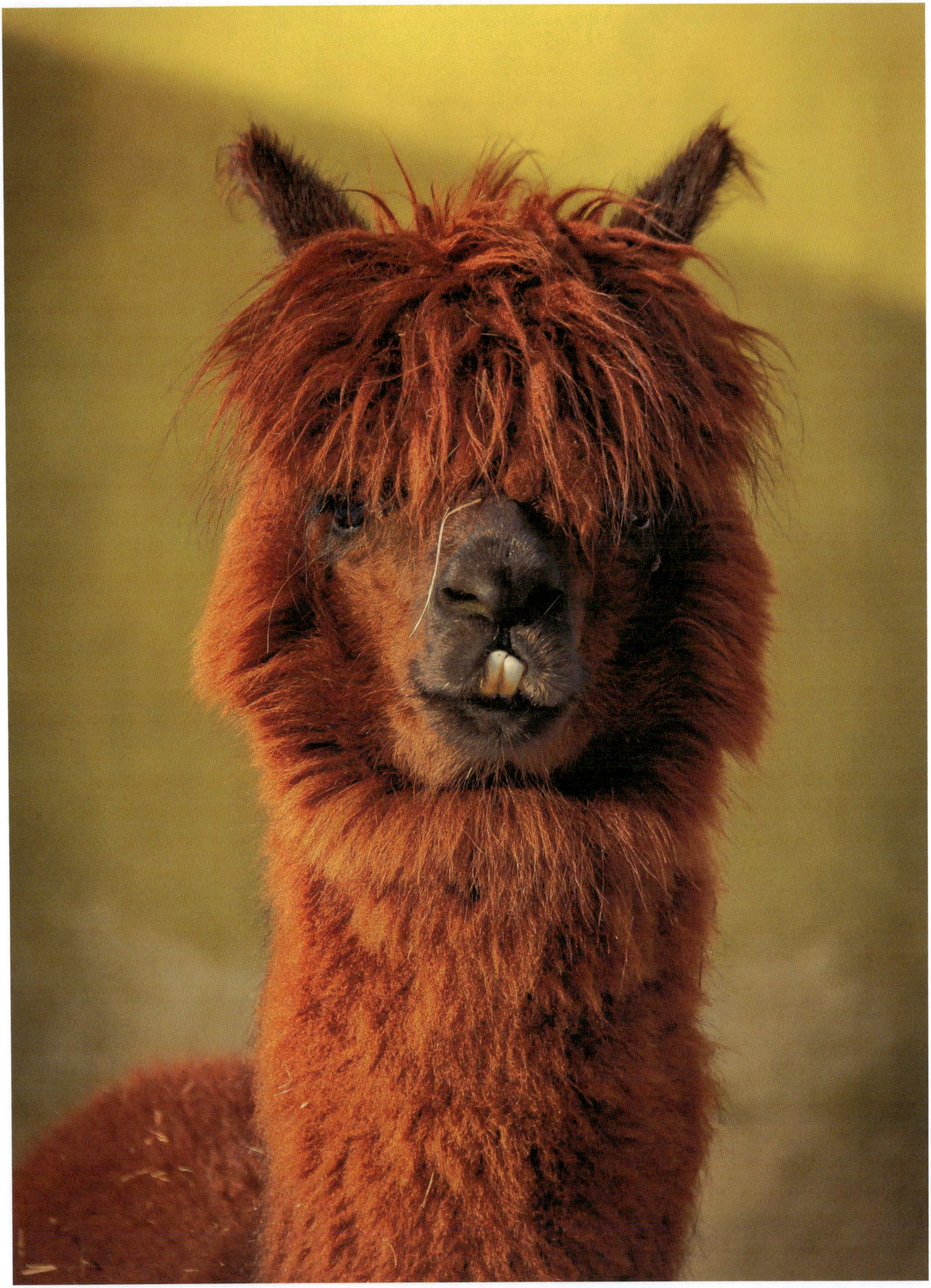

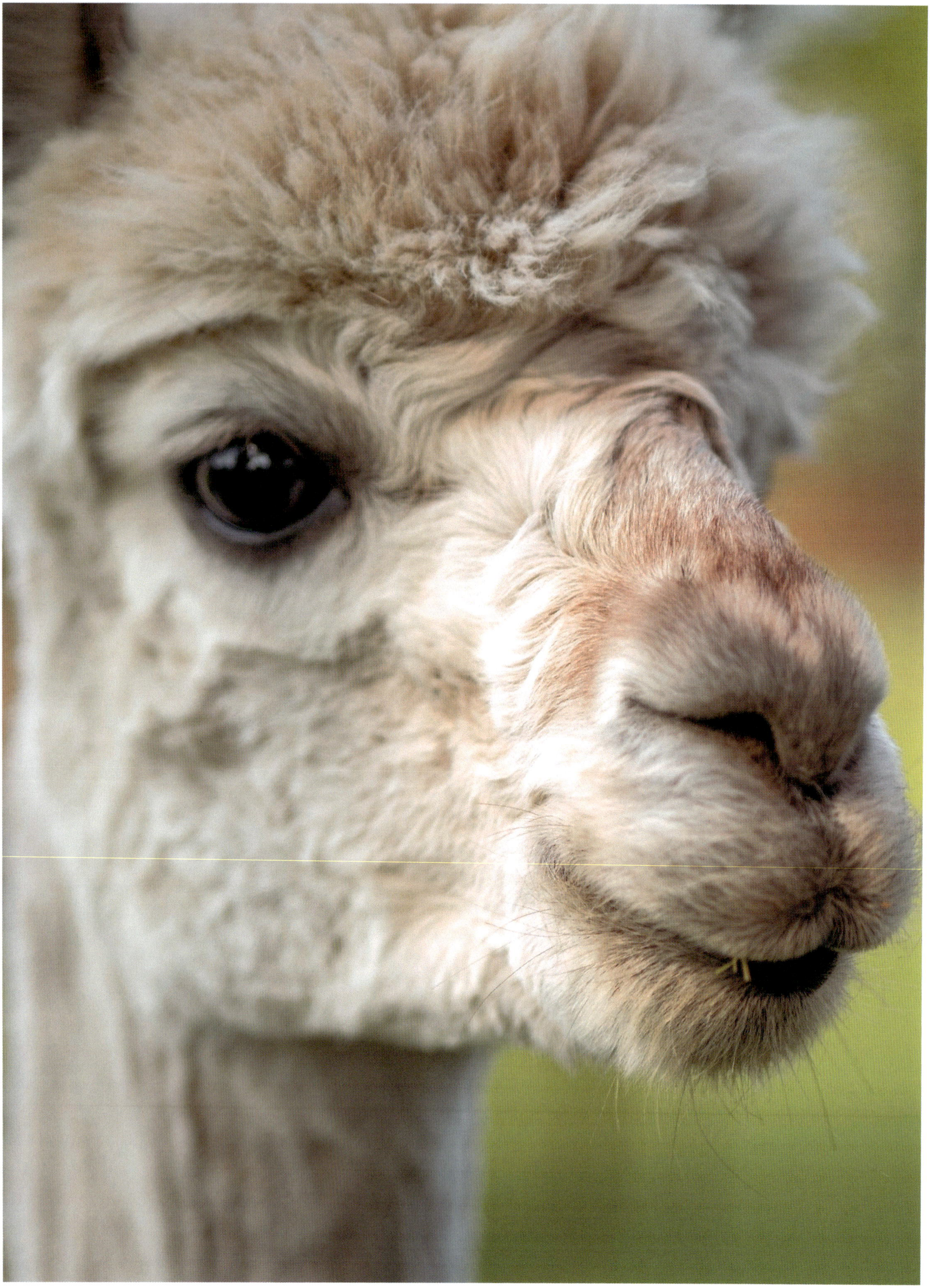

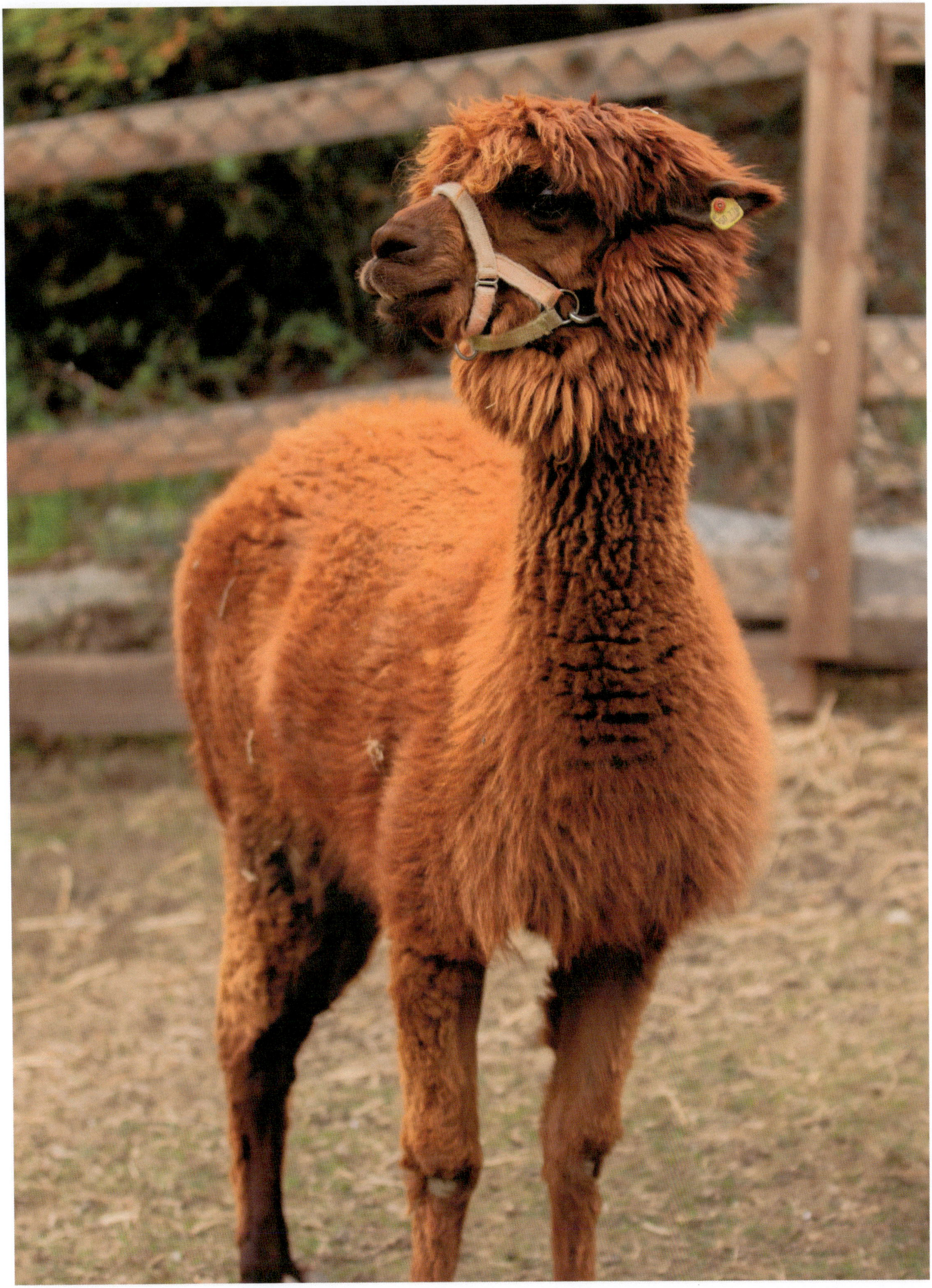

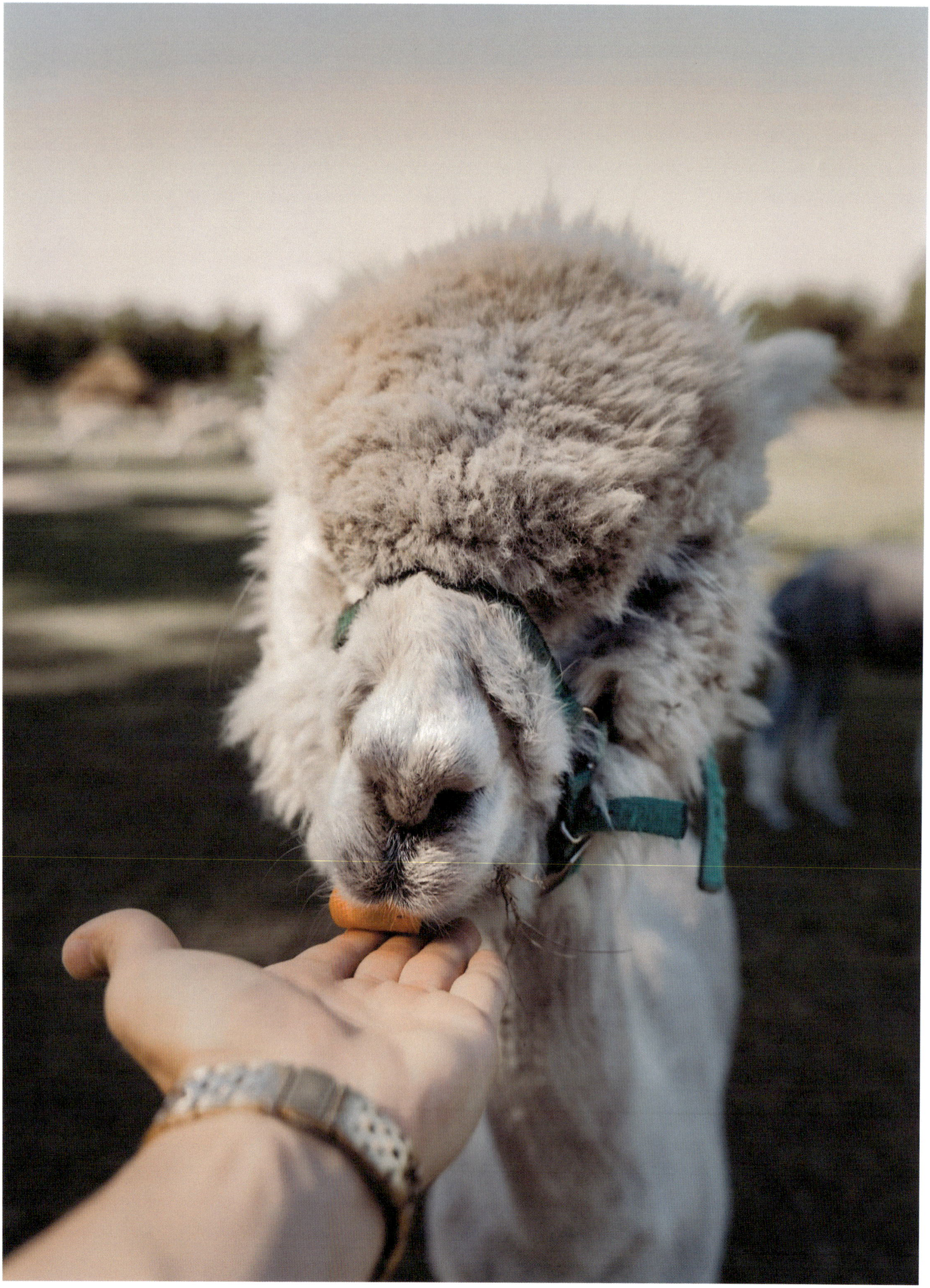

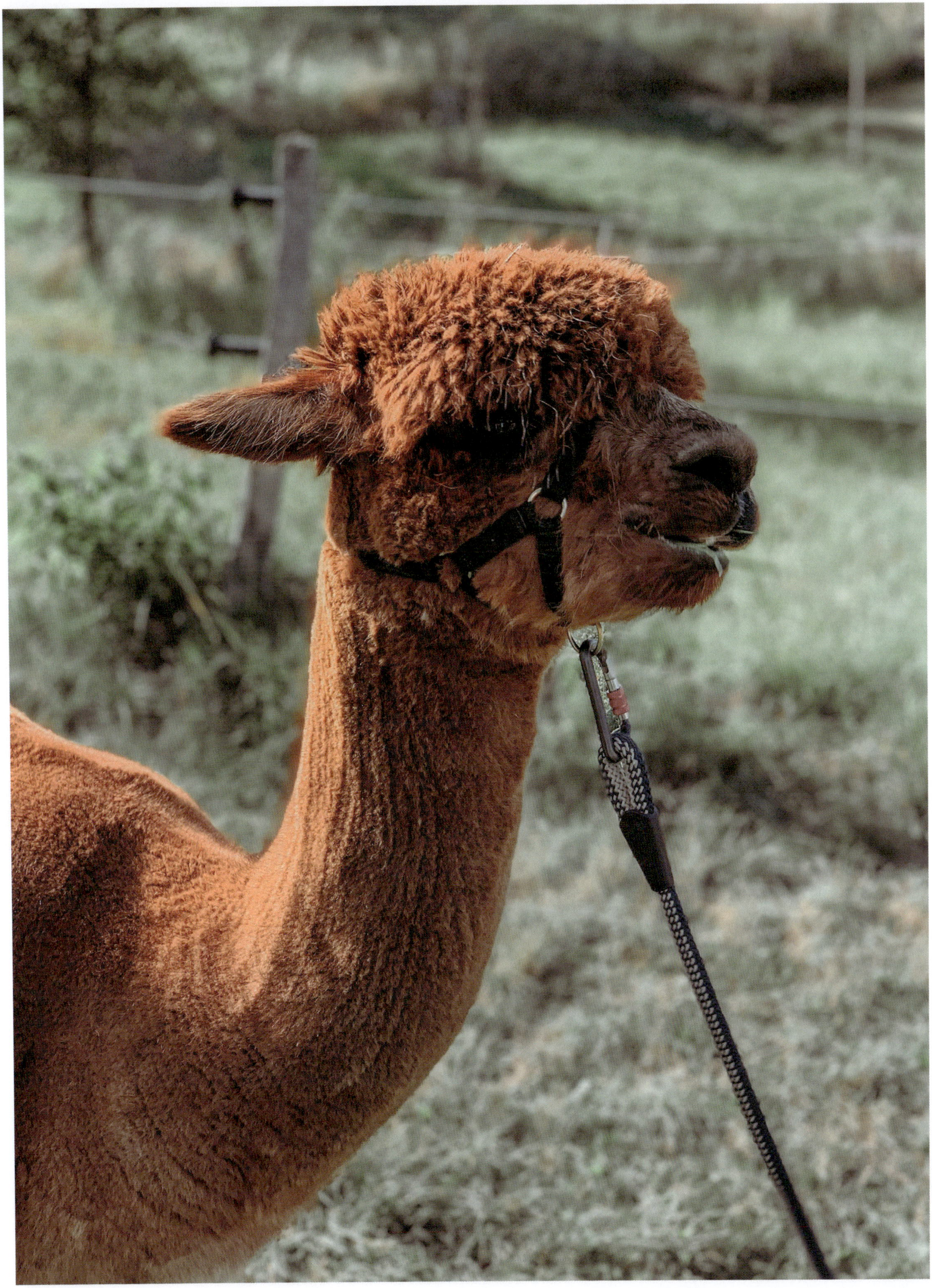

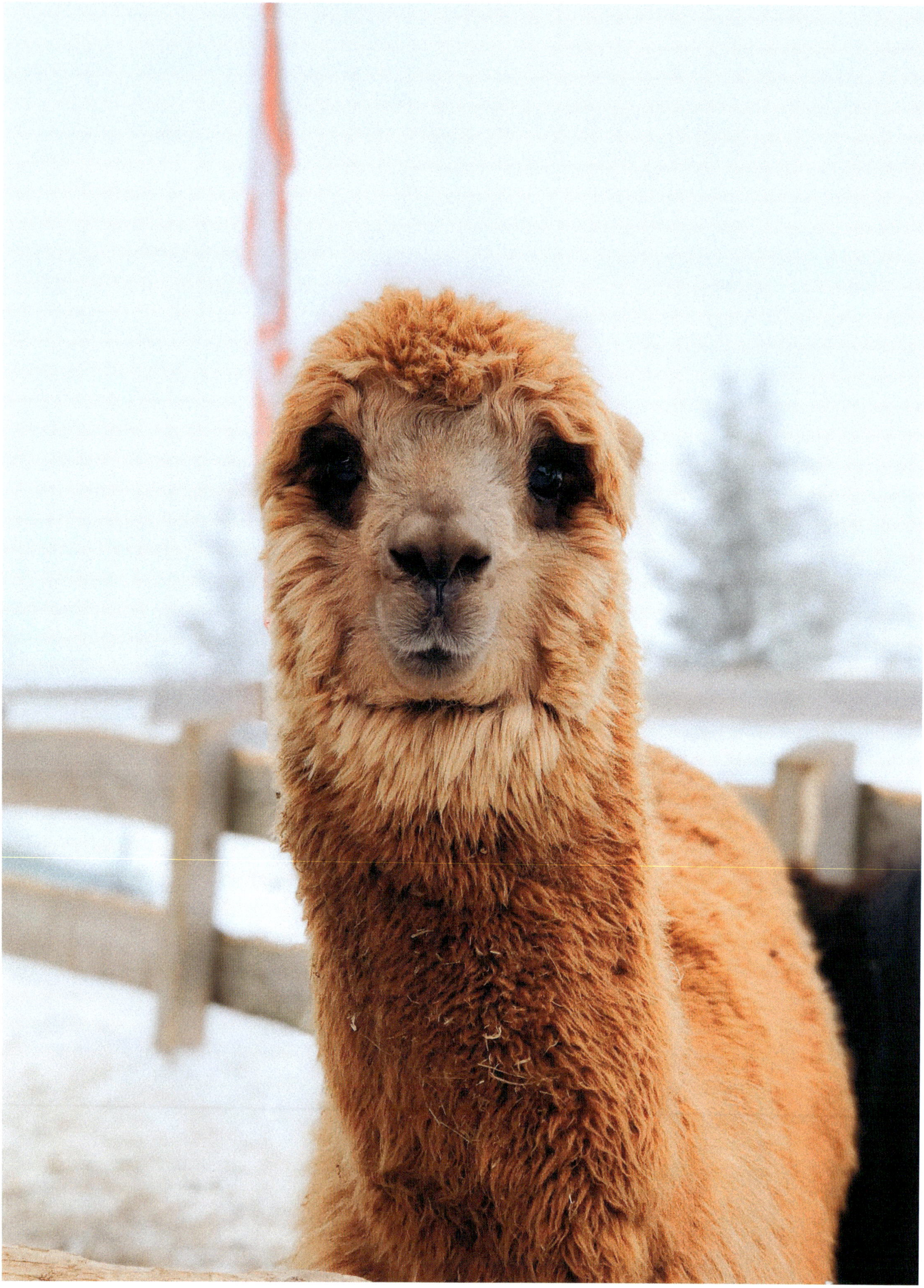

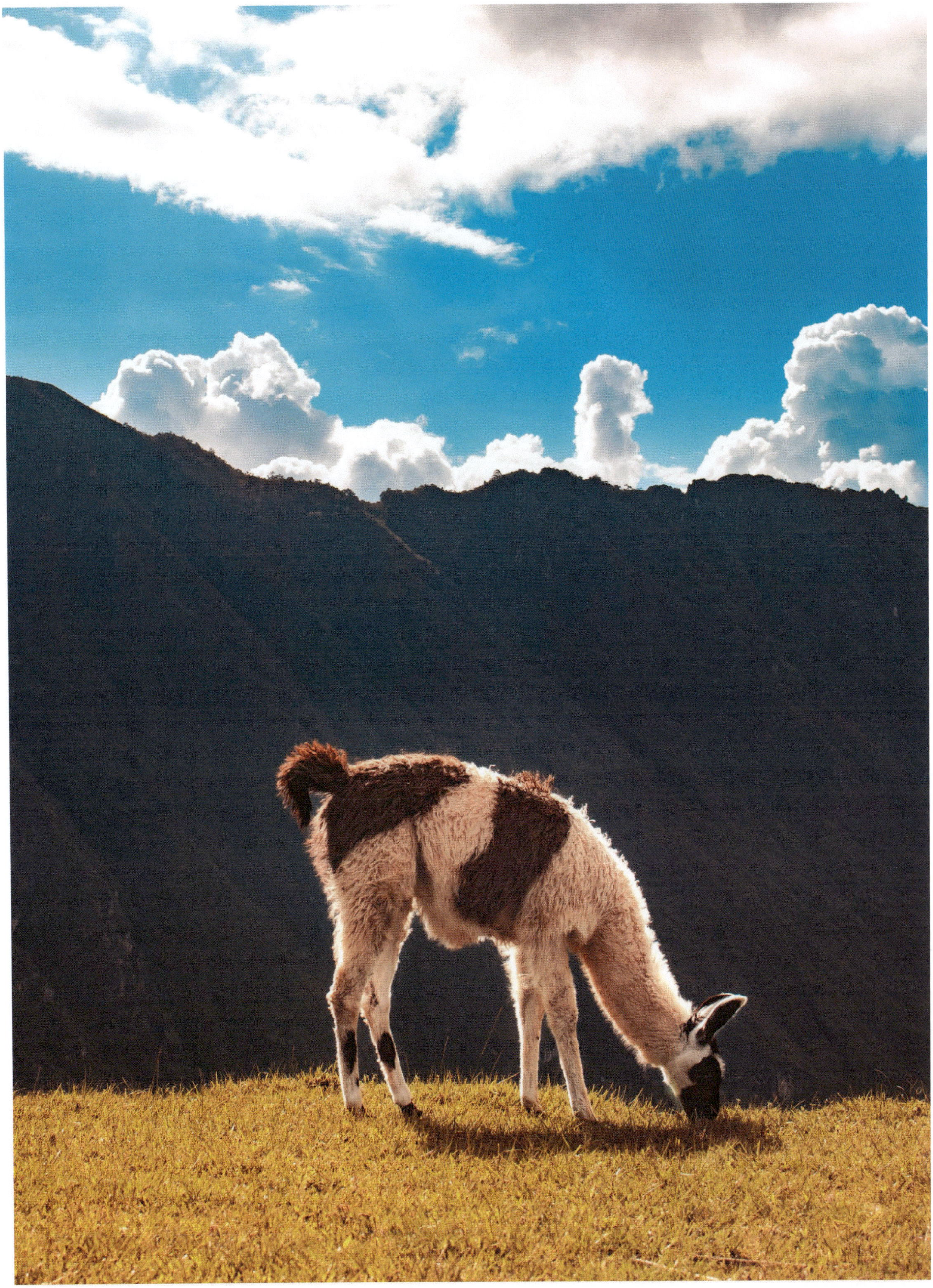

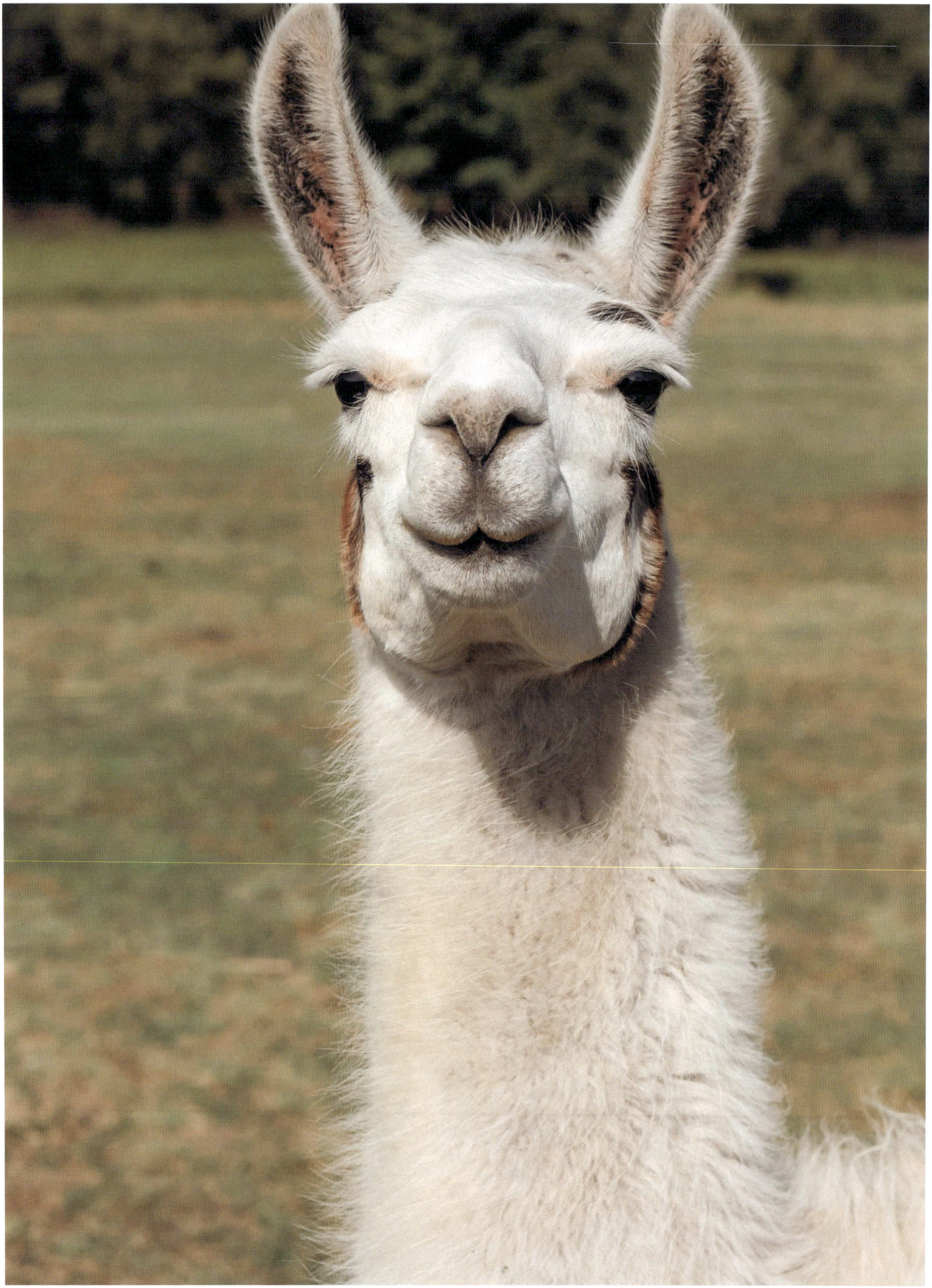

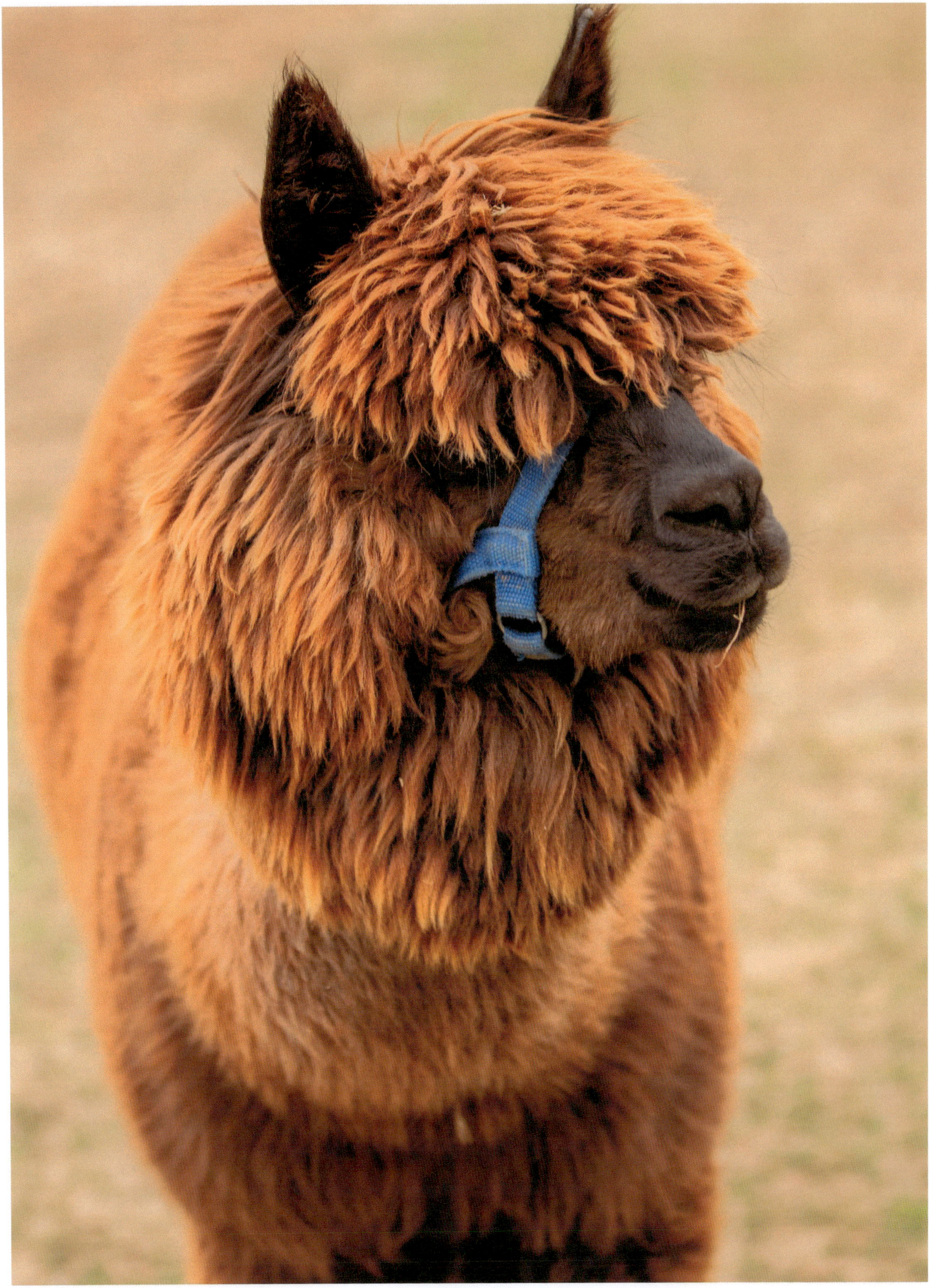

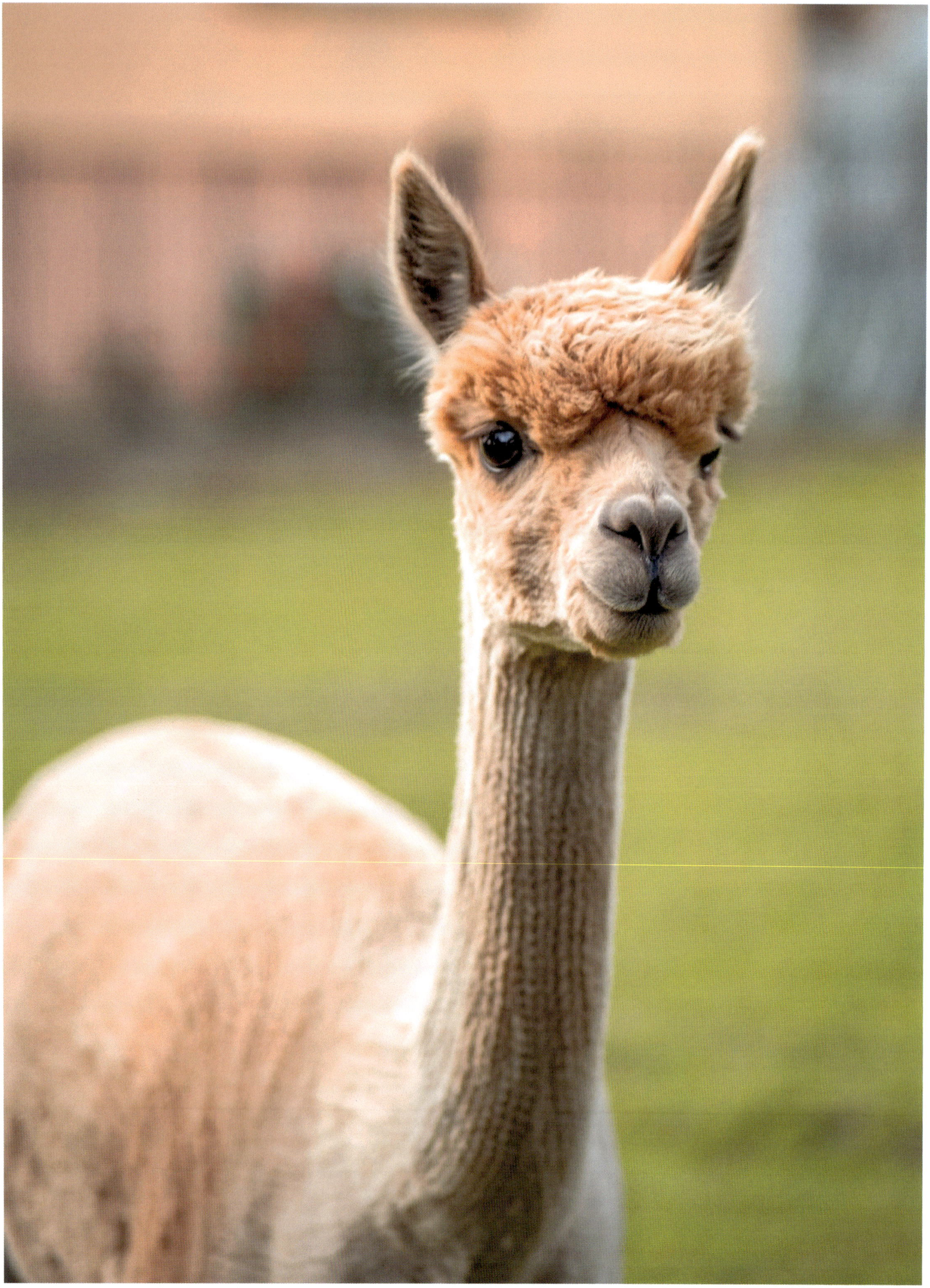

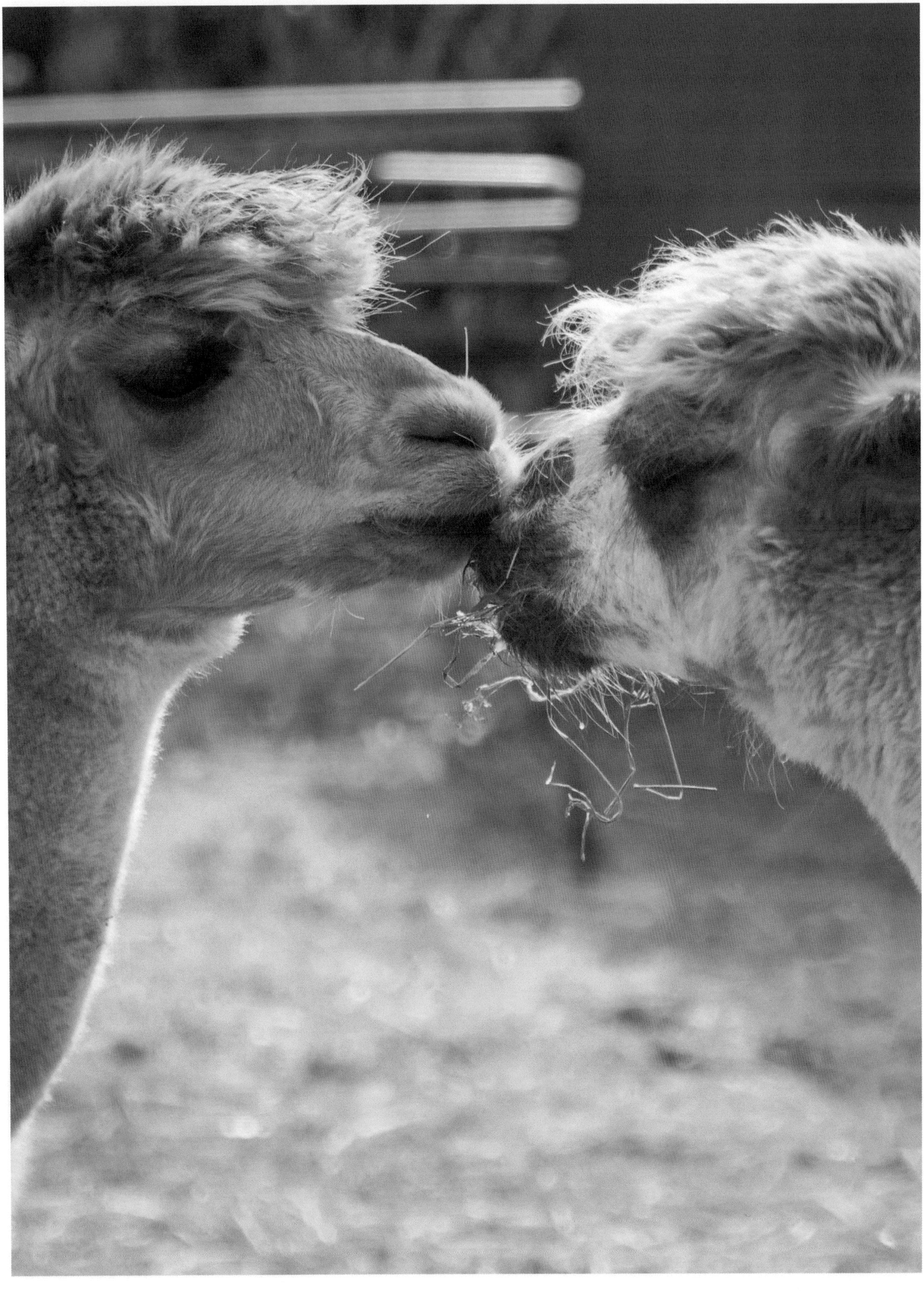

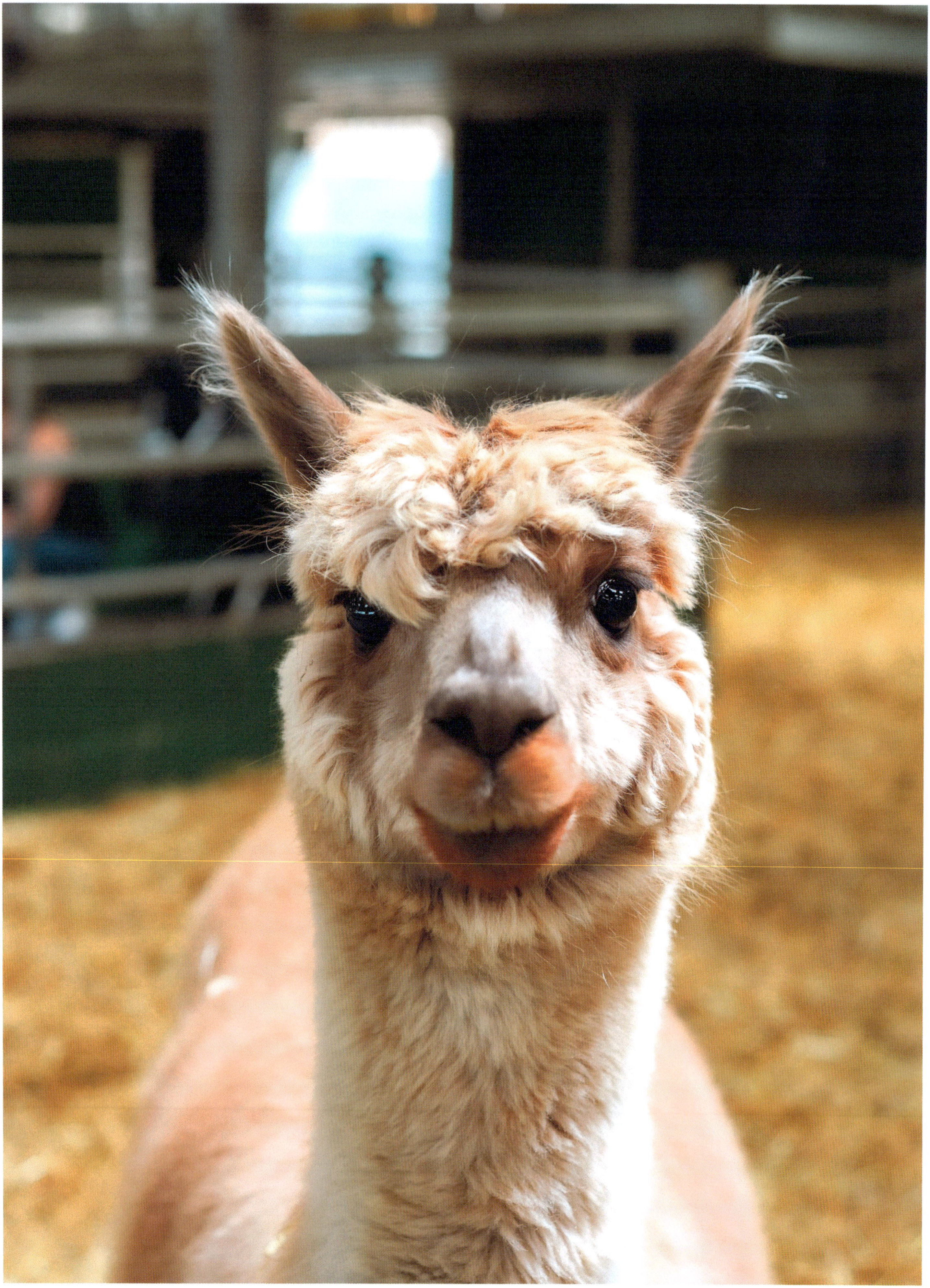

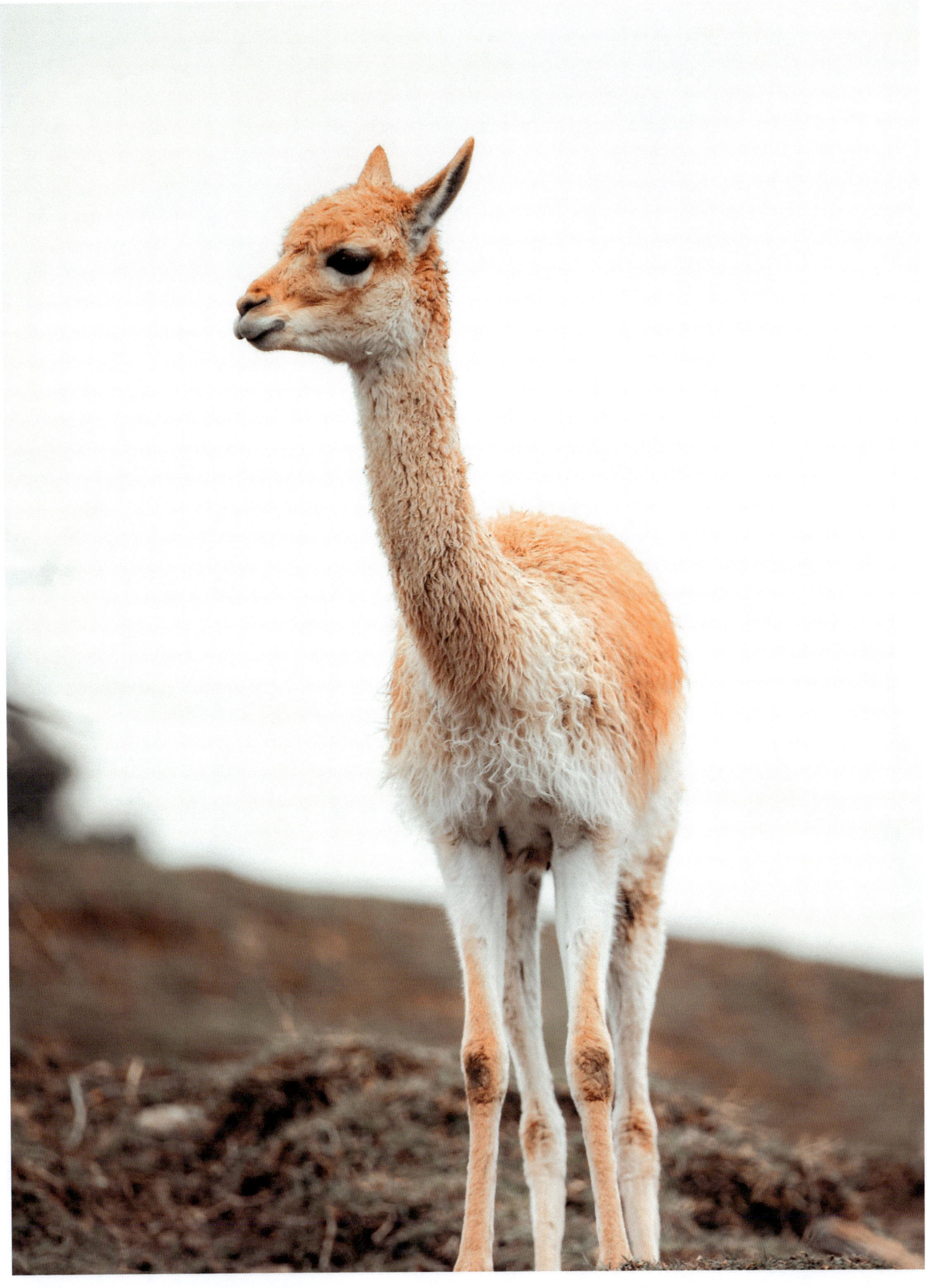

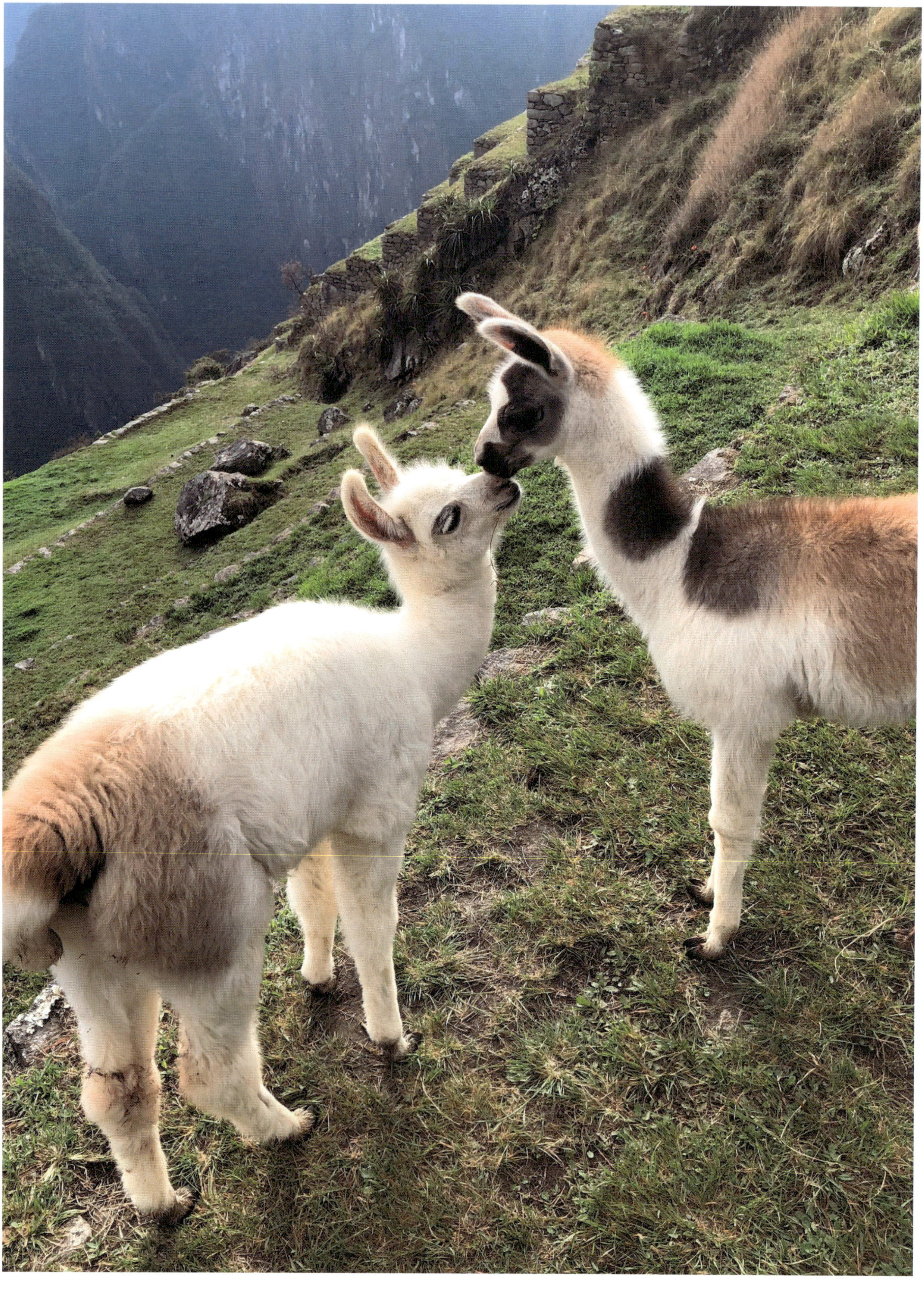

Printed in Great Britain
by Amazon

35536563R00025